Praise for Anne Fadiman's *Ex Libris*

"In the literary Eden that forms Anne Fadiman's life, the air remains pure allusion, the marginalia flows, and the only snake in the grass is a typo."
—Renee Tursi, *The New York Times Book Review*

"It is not just that she is erudite (which she is), or that an outlandish word will send her to the dictionary (which it will). It's that a book will set her pulses racing, whether it's Livy's account of the battle of Lake Trasimene or Beatrix Potter's 'The Story of the Fierce Bad Rabbit.' More to the point, perhaps, she can set ours racing too."
—*The Economist*

"Anne Fadiman reveals the delights of her bibliographic life, where reading, writing, and collecting books is not just a profession, but an abiding, self-affirming, and shared passion, thanks to her equally hooked-on-books husband."
—*Elle*

"These 18 stylish, dryly humorous essays . . . pay tribute to the joys of reading, the delights of language, and the quirks (yes, there are a few) of fellow bibliophiles . . . [A] charmingly uncommon miscellany on literary love."
—Megan Harlan, *Entertainment Weekly*

Anne Fadiman

Ex Libris

Anne Fadiman is the editor of *The American Scholar*. Recipient of a National Book Critics Circle Award for her first book, *The Spirit Catches You and You Fall Down* (FSG, 1997), she has written for *The New Yorker*, *Civilization*, *Harper's*, *Life*, and *The New York Times*, among other publications. She and her family recently moved from New York City to western Massachusetts.

Also by Anne Fadiman

The Spirit Catches You and You Fall Down

EX LIBRIS

CONFESSIONS OF A COMMON READER

ANNE FADIMAN

FARRAR, STRAUS AND GIROUX

NEW YORK

Farrar, Straus and Giroux
19 Union Square West, New York 10003

Distributed in Canada by Douglas & McIntyre Ltd.
Printed in the United States of America
Published in 1998 by Farrar, Straus and Giroux
First paperback edition, 2000
Second printing, 2001

Endpaper design by Jonathan D. Lippincott
Endpaper art composed by Fausta Tamburino from book pages
of the 1902 edition of the Sears, Roebuck Catalogue
Endpaper bookplate is an adaptation of a bookplate by Rockwell
Kent from the library of Elnita Straus, Council House

Library of Congress Cataloging-in-Publication Data
Fadiman, Anne, 1953–
    Ex libris : confessions of a common reader / Anne Fadiman.
    — 1st ed.
        p.   cm.
    ISBN 0-374-52722-9 (pbk.)
    1. Fadiman, Anne, 1953–   —Books and reading.   I. Title.
PN4874.F33   1998
814'.54—dc21   98-21109

The essays in this book appeared, in slightly different form, in *Civilization* magazine.

Designed by Jonathan D. Lippincott

For Clifton Fadiman
and Annalee Whitmore Jacoby Fadiman,
who built my ancestral castles

 CONTENTS

r /   e /

When the Irish novelist John McGahern was a child, his sisters unlaced and removed one of his shoes while he was reading. He did not stir. They placed a straw hat on his head. No response. Only when they took away the wooden chair on which he was sitting did he, as he puts it, "wake out of the book."

"Wake" is just the right verb, because there is a certain kind of child who awakens from a book as from an abyssal sleep, swimming heavily up through layers of consciousness toward a reality that seems less real than the dream-state that has been left behind. I was such a child. Later, as a teenager under the influence of Hardy, I could not fall in love without classifying the boy as a Damon or a Clym. Later still, I lay with my husband (a Clym) in a bed that was lumpy with books, hoping the delivery of our first child would resemble Kitty's birth scene in *Anna Karenina* but fearing it might be more like Mrs. Thingummy's in *Oliver Twist*.

I began to write *Ex Libris* when it occurred to me how curious it was that books are so often written about as if they were toasters. Is this brand of toaster better than that brand of toaster? At $24.95, is this toaster a best buy? There is nothing about how I may feel about my toaster ten years hence, and nothing about the tender feelings I may yet harbor for my old toaster. This model of readers as consumers—one I have abetted in many a book review myself—neatly omits what I consider the heart of reading: not whether we wish to purchase a new book but how we maintain our connections with our old books, the ones we have lived with for years, the ones whose textures and colors and smells have become as familiar to us as our children's skin.

In *The Common Reader*, Virginia Woolf (who borrowed her title from a phrase in Samuel Johnson's *Life of Gray*) wrote of "all those rooms, too humble to be called libraries, yet full of books, where the pursuit of reading is carried on by private people." The common reader, she said, "differs from the critic and the scholar. He is worse educated, and nature has not gifted him so generously. He reads for his own pleasure rather than to impart knowledge or correct the opinions of others. Above all, he is guided by an instinct to create for himself, out of whatever odds and ends he can come by, some kind of whole." This book is the whole that I have attempted to create from the thousands of odds and ends that crowd my sagging bookshelves.

I wrote these eighteen essays over a period of four years. They are presented here in the order in which they were written, with the exception of the last two, which have exchanged places. I have left the facts as they were; for example, William Kunstler was alive when I wrote about him, so he remains alive in these pages. Over the course of those years, my son was born, my daughter learned to read, my husband and I turned forty, my mother turned eighty, my father turned ninety. Our books, however— even the ones printed long before we were born—remained ageless. They recorded the passage of real time, and because they reminded us of all the occasions on which they had been read and reread, they also reflected the passage of the preceding decades.

Books wrote our life story, and as they accumulated on our shelves (and on our windowsills, and underneath our sofa, and on top of our refrigerator), they became chapters in it themselves. How could it be otherwise?

A.F.

Ex Libris

A few months ago, my husband and I decided to mix our books together. We had known each other for ten years, lived together for six, been married for five. Our mismatched coffee mugs cohabited amicably; we wore each other's T-shirts and, in a pinch, socks; and our record collections had long ago miscegenated without incident, my Josquin Desprez motets cozying up to George's *Worst of Jefferson Airplane*, to the enrichment, we believed, of both. But our libraries had remained separate, mine mostly at the north end of our loft, his at the south. We agreed that it made no sense for my *Billy Budd* to languish forty feet from his *Moby-Dick*, yet neither of us had lifted a finger to bring them together.

We had been married in this loft, in full view of our mutually quarantined Melvilles. Promising to love each other for richer or for poorer, in sickness and in health— even promising to forsake all others—had been no problem, but it was a good thing the *Book of Common Prayer* didn't say anything about marrying our libraries and throwing out the duplicates. That would have been a far more solemn vow, one that would probably have caused the wedding to grind to a mortifying halt. We were both writers, and we both invested in our books the kind of emotion most people reserve for their old love letters. Sharing a bed and a future was child's play compared to sharing my copy of *The Complete Poems of W. B. Yeats*, from which I had once read "Under Ben Bulben" aloud while standing at Yeats's grave in the Drumcliff churchyard, or George's copy of *T. S. Eliot's Selected Poems*, given to him in the ninth grade by his best friend, Rob Farnsworth, who inscribed it "Best Wishes from Gerry Cheevers." (Gerry Cheevers, one of Rob's nicknames, was the goalie of the Boston Bruins, and the inscription is probably unique, linking T. S. Eliot and ice hockey for the first time in history.)

Our reluctance to conjugate our Melvilles was also fueled by some essential differences in our characters. George is a lumper. I am a splitter. His books commingled democratically, united under the all-inclusive flag of Literature. Some were vertical, some horizontal, and some actually placed *behind* others. Mine were balkanized by nationality and subject matter. Like most people with a high tolerance for clutter, George maintains a basic trust in three-dimensional objects. If he wants something, he believes it will present itself, and therefore it usually does. I, on the other hand, believe that books, maps, scissors, and Scotch tape dispensers are all unreliable vagrants, likely to take off for parts unknown unless strictly confined to quarters. My books, therefore, have always been rigidly regimented.

After five years of marriage and a child, George and I finally resolved that we were ready for the more profound intimacy of library consolidation. It was unclear, however, how we were to find a meeting point between his English-garden approach and my French-garden one. At least in the short run, I prevailed, on the theory that he could find his books if they were arranged like mine but I could never find mine if they were arranged like his. We agreed to sort by topic—History, Psychology, Nature, Travel, and so on. Literature would be subdivided by nationality. (If George found this plan excessively finicky, at least he granted that it was a damn sight better than the system some friends of ours had told us about. Some friends of *theirs* had rented their house for several months to an interior decorator. When they returned, they discovered that their entire library had been reorganized by color and size. Shortly thereafter, the decorator met with a fatal automobile accident. I confess that when this story was told, everyone around the dinner table concurred that justice had been served.)

So much for the ground rules. We ran into trouble, however, when I announced my plan to arrange English literature chronologically but American literature alphabetically by author. My defense went like this: Our English collection spanned six centuries, and to shelve it chronologically would allow us to watch the broad sweep of literature unfold before our very eyes. The Victorians *be-*

longed together; separating them would be like breaking up a family. Besides, Susan Sontag arranged *her* books chronologically. She had told *The New York Times* that it would set her teeth on edge to put Pynchon next to Plato. So there. Our American collection, on the other hand, was mostly twentieth-century, much of it so recent that chronological distinctions would require Talmudic hairsplitting. Ergo, alphabetization. George eventually caved in, but more for the sake of marital harmony than because of a true conversion. A particularly bad moment occurred while he was in the process of transferring my Shakespeare collection from one bookcase to another and I called out, "Be sure to keep the plays in chronological order!"

"You mean we're going to be chronological *within each author*?" he gasped. "But no one even knows for sure when Shakespeare wrote his plays!"

"Well," I blustered, "we know he wrote *Romeo and Juliet* before *The Tempest*. I'd like to see that reflected on our shelves."

George says that was one of the few times he has seriously contemplated divorce.

Our transfer of books across the Mason-Dixon Line that separated my northern shelves from his southern ones took about a week. Every night we lined up books on the floor, interlarding mine with his before putting them on the shelves, which meant that for a week we had to hopscotch over hundreds of volumes in order to get from bathroom to kitchen to bedroom. We physically handled—fondled, really—every book we owned. Some had inscriptions from old lovers. Some had inscriptions from each other. Some were like time capsules: my *Major British Writers* contained a list of poets required for my 1970 twelfth-grade English final; a postcard with a ten-cent stamp dropped out of George's copy of *On the Road*.

As our piles accumulated on the floor, we had several heated debates about not just which books should go together but where they should go. I had lived in the loft for nine years before George moved in, and English literature had always occupied the most public spot, the wall facing the front door. (At the opposite end of the spectrum was a small bookshelf with a door, to the right of my desk, behind which lurked *The Zipcode Directory* and *The Complete Scarsdale Diet*.) George thought American literature deserved this place of honor instead. If I agreed to present myself to the world as an acolyte of A. J. Liebling rather than of Walter Pater, I would be admitting that the academic I had once thought I'd be had forever been replaced by the journalist I had become. Deciding that this was the truth and that, furthermore, our entrance wall should represent my husband as well as myself, I capitulated, but with a lump in my throat.

In the shelves next to our bed, we created a new category: Books by Friends and Relatives. I'd gotten the idea from a writer friend (now represented on these shelves

herself) who had done the same, saying it gave her a warm
feeling to have so many of the people she loved gathered
together in one place. George was initially dubious. He felt
it was potentially insulting, for example, to banish Mark
Helprin from the American literature canon, where he had
once reposed alphabetically next to Ernest Hemingway,
and force him to bed down instead with Peter Lerangis,
the author, under a female pseudonym, of sixteen volumes
of *The Baby-Sitters Club*. (Eventually he changed his mind,
deciding that Mark and Peter might actually find a good
deal to say to one another.)

By far the hardest task came toward the end of the week,
when we sorted through our duplicates and decided whose
to keep. I realized that we had both been hoarding redundant copies of our favorite books "just in case" we ever
split up. If George got rid of his beat-up copy of *To the
Lighthouse* and I said goodbye to my genital-pink paperback of *Couples*, read so often in my late teens (when Updike's explorations of the complexities of marriage seemed
unimaginably exotic) that it had sundered into a triptych
held together with a rubber band—well, then we would
clearly have to stick together for good. Our bridges would
be burned.

We each owned copies of about fifty books in common.
We decided that hardbacks would prevail over paperbacks
unless the paperbacks contained marginalia. We kept my
Middlemarch, read at eighteen, in which were registered
my nascent attempts at literary criticism (page 37: "Grrr";

page 261: "Bullshit"; page 294: "Yccch"); George's *Magic Mountain*; my *War and Peace*. *Women in Love* generated the most agonizing discussion. George had read it at sixteen. He insisted that whenever he reread it, no edition other than his original Bantam paperback, with its psychedelic cover of one nude and one seminude woman, would possibly do. I had read it at eighteen. I kept no diary that year, but I had no need of one to remind me that that was the year I lost my virginity. It was all too apparent from the comments I wrote in my Viking edition (page 18: "Violence substitute for sex"; page 154: "Sexual pain"; page 159: "Sexual power"; page 158: "Sex"). What could we do but throw in the towel and keep both copies?

After a final, post-midnight push, we were done. Our duplicates, plus another hundred or so painful culls, were neatly stacked, ready to be carted off to Goodwill. Sweating and panting beneath our triumphantly united Melvilles, we kissed.

Our library was in impeccable order, but it was a little airless, much as my own life had been before George entered it. And so, by subtle degrees, as the weeks passed, George's style began to retake the upper hand in a not entirely unwelcome fashion. As the excessively rectilinear foundation lines of a new house are softened by the addition of a few windblown weeds here, a knocked-over tricycle there, so the flawlessness of our new system was softened by the forces of entropy and my husband, which are closely allied. Our bedside tables started to sag under the weight of new, unsorted volumes. The Shakespeares reshuffled. One day I noticed that the *Iliad* and *The Decline and Fall of the Roman Empire* had somehow found their way to the Friends and Relatives section. Confronted with the evidence, George crossed his fingers and said, "Well, Gibbon and I were like *that*."

A couple of weeks ago, when George was out of town, I decided to reread *Travels with Charley*. I got into bed with the copy I had first read the summer I turned seventeen. I was settling into the familiar feel of my crumbly old paperback, the one with Steinbeck sitting cross-legged next to his poodle on the cover, when I reached page 192. There, next to a passage about the dwindling redwood forests of California, in a younger version of my husband's handwriting—I'd recognize it anywhere—was the plaintive comment "Why do we destroy the environment?"

We must have had identical copies, and we'd kept George's. My books and his books had become our books. We were really married.

When my older brother, Kim, and I were children, our father used to tell us stories about a bookworm named Wally. Wally, a squiggly little vermicule with a red baseball cap, didn't merely like books. He ate them. The monosyllables he found in most children's books failed to satisfy his voracious appetite, so he turned instead to the dictionary, which offered a richer bill of fare. In *Wally the Wordworm*, a chronicle of some of our hero's lexicographic adventures that my father wrote when I was eleven, Wally savored such high-calorie morsels as *syzygy, ptarmigan*—which tasted pterrible at first, until he threw away the *p*—and *sesquipedalian*, which looks as if it means "long word" and, in fact, does. Inspired by Wally, Kim and I spent years vying to see who could find the best sesquipedalian. Kim won with *paradimethylaminobenzaldehyde*, a smelly chemical that we used to sing to the tune of "The Irish Washerwoman."

One of my greatest disappointments about growing up

is that it has become harder and harder to achieve a Wally-like degree of sesquipedalian repletion. There just aren't enough new words. Or so I thought until last summer, when I happened to read a book called *The Tiger in the House*, written in 1920 by Carl Van Vechten, a novelist and jazz critic whose prose style, if not actually purple, can certainly be described as mauve. Its subject was cats—cats in literature, history, music, art, and so on. I was writing an article about cats myself, and I'd read several recent compendia of cat lore that covered much the same territory. The authors of these books made only one assumption about their readers: that they were interested in cats. Van Vechten, by contrast, assumed that his readers were on in-timate terms with classical mythology and the Bible; that they could read music (he included part of the score from Domenico Scarlatti's "Cat's Fugue"); and that they were familiar with hundreds of writers, artists, and composers to whom he referred by last name only, as if Sacchini and Teniers needed as little introduction as Bach and Rembrandt.

What simultaneously most thrilled me and made me feel most like a dunce was Van Vechten's vocabulary. I couldn't remember the last time I'd met so many words I didn't know. By the end of the book I'd jotted down twenty-two. Not only did I have no idea what they meant, I couldn't remember even *seeing* them before. They might as well have been Old Norse. Here is the list: *monophysite, me-phitic, calineries, diapason, grimoire, adapertile, retromin-*

gent, perllan, cupellation, adytum, sepoy, subadar, paludal, apozemical, camorra, ithyphallic, alcalde, aspergill, agathodemon, kakodemon, goetic, and *opopanax.* These words didn't require a wordworm. They required a word anaconda.

Carl Van Vechten, who is better remembered as a patron of the Harlem Renaissance than as a cat apologist, wrote letters to his literary co-saloniers on stationery that bore the motto "A little too much is just enough for me." His weakness for over-the-top vocabulary (along with over-the-top everything else) was notorious. However, I doubt his book would have gone through four printings if his original readers had found these words as inscrutable as I did. My guess is that in 1920, educated general readers would have considered my list difficult but not impossible. Many of them would have known Greek and Latin, which would have provided etymological clues to about half the list; and seventy-five years ago, several words that now sound creakily archaic had not yet acquired a layer of dust. Sepoys and subadars, for instance—two ranks of Indian soldiers—still served the British administration. The camorra, a Mafia-like secret society, still kidnapped tourists in Naples. Aspergills, brushes used to sprinkle holy water, were still routinely used in Catholic masses. People still washed themselves with soap made with oil of opopanax, a fragrant plant.

Feeling elegiac about the lost world conjured up by Van Vechten's words, I tried them out on my family, to see if Wally's other former acolytes found them any more familiar than I did. (If any readers wish to grill themselves, the meanings of the words not defined during the course of this essay can be found on page 19.) Warming to the task, I was about to subject my friends to the killer quiz when my editor, who had no desire to become a victim himself, said gently, "Hold your horses, Anne. Not everyone loves tests as much as you do."

He had a point. When I was growing up, not only did my family walk around spouting sesquipedalians, but we viewed all forms of intellectual competition as a sacrament, a kind of holy water, as it were, to be slathered on at every opportunity with the largest possible aspergill. When I saw the movie *Quiz Show*, I squirmed in my seat because the literary-hothouse atmosphere of the Van Doren ménage was all too familiar. Like the young Van Dorens, the Fadiman children were ritually asked to identify literary quotations. While my mother negotiated a honking traffic jam on a Los Angeles freeway en route to a restaurant, my father would mutter, " 'We are here as on a darkling plain / Swept with confused alarms of struggle and flight.' Source?" And Kim and I would squeal in chorus, " 'Dover Beach'!"

Our competitive fervor reached its apogee every Sunday afternoon, when we gathered around the television set for our weekly round of *G.E. College Bowl*. As you may remember if you are of a certain age and disposition, this was a quiz show—an honest, unrigged one—in which two teams of four students, each representing a different college, competed for scholarship money. Our family also constituted a team of four, which—I am admitting this in public for the very first time—we called Fadiman U. It was an article of faith in our home that Fadiman U. could beat any other U., and indeed, in five or six years of competition, we lost only to Brandeis and Colorado College. My father knew the answers to all the history and literature questions. My mother knew politics and sports. My brother knew science. I rarely knew anything that another member of Fadiman U. didn't know as well, but I had quicker reflexes than my parents, so sometimes I managed to bang the arm of my chair (our home-team version of pressing the College Bowl buzzer) first. Fadiman U. always yelled out the answer before Robert Earle, the M.C., could even finish asking the question. "Wing Biddlebaum is an unfortunate ex-schoolteacher. Dr. Percival is—" WHOMP! "*Winesburg, Ohio!*" "After being poisoned and shot several times—" WHOMP! "Rasputin!"

Having spent my childhood struggling to one-up my family, I found it quite liberating to present the rest of the Fadiman camorra with a vocabulary test that I myself had resoundingly flunked—*pre*-flunked, before their hands could even get close to their chair arms. My mother knew one word, *sepoy*. My brother, in a humbling sibling shut-out, knew nine: *mephitic*, *monophysite*, *diapason*, *sepoy*, *subadar*, *alcalde*, *aspergill*, *agathodemon*, and *kakodemon*. My father knew twelve: all the ones Kim knew (with the exception of *aspergill*), plus *retromingent*, *paludal*, *camorra*, and *opopanax*. WHOMP!

My husband, even though he views the Fadiman U.

ethos as a dangerous psychosis, cheerfully submitted to my catechism as well. He knew *diapason*. I think he was quite pleased to beat me. Ignoring my editor's warning, I then proceeded to poll a random sampling of my friends: a movie critic, a freelance writer, three editors, a playwright, an English professor, a classics professor, a lawyer, a law student, a stand-up comic, and the director of operations for the New York City bus system. Some of them tried to wriggle out of the competition by treating the quiz as a game of Dictionary, with trumped-up definitions (*paludal*: "a German pastry made from a lapdog"; *subadar*: "a Turkish spittoon"; *grimoire*: "where Bluebeard stored his bathrobe"). The final results: five zeros, three 1s, one 2, three 7s, and one 9.

Although I cannot claim that my poll was statistically significant, it did strike me that, glossologically speaking, my respondents were either on the bus or off the bus: they knew hardly any words, or they knew a lot. What set the Wallys apart? My father, of course—the champion to date—*is* Wally, and therefore occupies a class by himself, though I would also venture that he was aided by being ninety years old, and thus an intellectual product of the same era that shaped Carl Van Vechten. My lawyer friend, who knew seven words, restricts his reading almost entirely to works published before World War I. He is forty-one, but he might as well be ninety. The classics professor (9) and one of the editors (7) know Greek and Latin. My brother has the unparalleled advantage of owning no television set. Every one of the high scorers considered these twenty-two words—especially the ones they *didn't* know —not a prickly obstacle but a precious trove. "When you found them, you must have felt like stout Cortez!" exclaimed the English professor (7). ("Source?" I thought automatically. " 'On First Looking into Chapman's Homer.' ")

All the Wallys could remember exactly where they had encountered the words they knew. The English professor said, "*Mephitic!* That must mean foul-smelling. I've seen it in *Paradise Lost*, describing the smell of hell." My brother, a mountain guide and natural history teacher who lives in Wyoming, said, "*Mephitic*, hmm, yes. The scientific name for the striped skunk is *Mephitis mephitis*, which means *Stinky stinky.*" The lawyer, who, incredibly, had bumped into *mephitic* just the previous week in Carlyle's *Sartor Resartus*, possessed particularly vigorous powers of memory. When I asked him to define *monophysite*, he said, "That's a heretic, of course, who believes there is a single nature in the person of Christ. I first encountered it in *The Decline and Fall of the Roman Empire*, of which I read an abridged version in a green Dell Laurel edition with a picture of Roman ruins on the cover that I bought with my allowance for seventy-five cents when I was in grade school, at the bookstore at the corner of Mill Road and Peninsula Boulevard in Valley Stream, New York. I read it while walking home. It was springtime, and all the trees on Mill Road were in bud." No man ever remembered the face, dress, and perfume of an old lover with fonder precision than Jon remembered that glorious day when he and *monophysite* first met.

I asked my pollees whether they thought we know more words or fewer than we would have in 1920. They split right down the middle. "I bet we know at least as many," said the comic (0). "The new vocabulary of the Internet alone has easily made up for everything we've lost from nineteenth-century literature." I found this idea positively mephitic. The playwright (1) said sadly, "We know fewer words, and the ones we know are less beautiful. Just listen to the words on your list! The words we've lost tend to be connotative, and the ones we've gained tend to be denotative. I've never seen *modem* used in a poem." I share the playwright's views. I can bid farewell to *cupellation* (the act of assaying gold or silver from lead in a small, flat vessel called a cupel) without tears, but I regret that I have spent my life until now without knowing that a grimoire is a book of magic spells, or that an adytum is the inner sanctum of a temple. Wally's dictionary and Carl Van Vechten's cat book are grimoires. I feel their spells working on me at this very moment.

These twenty-two words, which two months ago were utter strangers, have now penetrated deeply into my own psychological adytum. Shortly after my daughter's fifth birthday party, I dreamed that instead of playing pin-the-tail-on-the-donkey, Susannah (who is now an aficionada of *Wally the Wordworm* herself) and her friends had played with my words, which had assumed shimmering three-dimensional shapes. Their favorite was *opopanax*. The children batted their new playthings delightedly back and forth, for the words were bright and pretty. But like balloons, they were excessively buoyant, and if you weren't careful, they floated away.

Calineries (n.), cajoleries; *diapason* (n.), full range of a voice or instrument; *adapertile* (adj.), easily openable; *retromingent* (adj.), urinating backward; *perilan* (n.), Welsh orchard; *paludal* (adj.), marshy or malarial; *apozemical* (adj.), infused; *ithyphallic* (adj.), having an erect penis; *alcalde* (n.), Spanish or Portuguese magistrate; *agatho-demon* (n.), good spirit; *kakodemon* (n.), evil spirit; *goetic* (adj.), pertaining to witchcraft.

It has long been my belief that everyone's library contains an Odd Shelf. On this shelf rests a small, mysterious corpus of volumes whose subject matter is completely unrelated to the rest of the library, yet which, upon closer inspection, reveals a good deal about its owner. George Orwell's Odd Shelf held a collection of bound sets of ladies' magazines from the 1860s, which he liked to read in his bathtub. Philip Larkin had an especially capacious Odd Shelf crammed with pornography, with an emphasis on spanking. Vice Admiral James Stockdale, having heard that Frederick the Great had never embarked on a campaign without his copy of *The Encheiridion*, brought to Vietnam the complete works of Epictetus, whose Stoic philosophy was to sustain him through eight years as a prisoner of war.

My own Odd Shelf holds sixty-four books about polar exploration: expedition narratives, journals, collections of photographs, works of natural history, and naval manuals

("Do not touch cold metal with moist bare hands. If you should inadvertently stick a hand to cold metal, urinate on the metal to warm it and save some inches of skin. If you stick both hands, you'd better have a friend along"). These books are so charged with sentiment that they might as well be smudged with seal blubber and soaked with spray from the Weddell Sea. My interest is a lonely one. I cannot trot it out at cocktail parties. I feel sometimes as if I have spent a large part of my life learning a dead language that no one I know can speak. Reading in bed, I will say to George, "Did you know that on Scott's first Antarctic expedition, Edward Wilson got up at one and five every morning to premasticate seal meat and stuff it down the throat of the pet emperor penguin chick he had captured on the Great Ice Barrier?" George will grunt. He is a rainforest man himself. He likes to dream of sitting under a giant tropical tree, his shoulders festooned with decaying lianas and sprouting bromeliads, with five hundred species of multicolored slugs dropping on his head. I consider his ideal landscape messy and hyperbolic—*too much*. He considers *my* ideal landscape, a white-on-white monochrome of seracs and crevasses with a single polar bear in the distance, chilly and parsimonious—*not enough*. I have tried to explain to him that the polar ethos has the same appeal as the body of Katharine Hepburn (something I know he holds in high esteem), which Spencer Tracy, in *Pat and Mike*, characterized thus: "Not much meat on 'er, but what there is is *cherce*."

My ardor for the choice minimalism of extreme latitudes began so early that it would take years on an analyst's couch to exhume its roots. I cannot remember a time when I did not prefer winter to summer, *The Snow Queen* to *Cinderella*, Norse myths to Greek. When I was thirteen or fourteen, I read C. S. Lewis's recollection of the central epiphany of his childhood, the moment he stumbled across a Norse-influenced poem by Longfellow that began with the lines

> *I heard a voice, that cried,*
> *"Balder the Beautiful*
> *Is dead, is dead!"*

"I knew nothing about Balder," wrote Lewis, "but instantly I was uplifted into huge regions of northern sky, [and] I desired with almost sickening intensity something never to be described (except that it is cold, spacious, severe, pale and remote)." When I read that passage, I shivered with a combination of sympathetic hypothermia and passionate recognition.

As I grew up, my yearning for what Lewis called Northernness (the Arctic) begat an antipodal yearning for Southernness (the Antarctic). Neither ultima Thule was easily accessible, so for a time I worked as a mountaineering instructor, on the theory that high altitudes were a reasonable substitute for high latitudes. A few years later, I managed to persuade a softhearted editor to send me twice to the

Arctic, once to write about polar bears and once about musk oxen. Each time I feared that my protracted pre-imaginings would poison the reality; each time the reality went one better. And each time, as soon as I returned home, I ran to my Odd Shelf, which instantly uplifted me back into Lewis's huge regions of northern sky. It was in this way that, over time, my crush on Balder the Beautiful was converted into a crush on Ross, Franklin, Nares, Shackleton, Oates, and Scott.

I should mention that all of the above explorers were unqualified failures. Not coincidentally, they were also all British. Americans admire success. Englishmen admire heroic failure. Given a choice—at least in my reading— I'm un-American enough to take quixotry over efficiency any day. I have always found the twilight-of-an-empire aspect of the Victorian age inexpressibly poignant, and no one could be more Victorian than the brave, earnest, optimistic, self-sacrificing, patriotic, honorable, high-minded, and utterly inept men who left their names all over the maps of the Arctic and Antarctic, yet failed to navigate the Northwest Passage and lost the races to both Poles. Who but an Englishman, Lieutenant William Edward Parry, would have decided, on reaching western Greenland, to wave a flag painted with an olive branch in order to ensure a peaceful first encounter with the polar Eskimos, who not only had never seen an olive branch but had never seen a *tree*? Who but an Englishman, the legendary Sir John Franklin, could have managed to die of starvation and

scurvy along with all 129 of his men in a region of the
Canadian Arctic whose game had supported an Eskimo col-
ony for centuries? When the corpses of some of Franklin's
officers and crew were later discovered, miles from their
ships, the men were found to have left behind their guns
but to have lugged such essentials as monogrammed silver
cutlery, a backgammon board, a cigar case, a clothes brush,
a tin of button polish, and a copy of *The Vicar of Wakefield*.
These men may have been incompetent bunglers, but, by
God, they were gentlemen.

The successful explorers—Roald Amundsen, for example, the ultrapragmatic Norwegian who sledged 830 miles
to the South Pole, killed and ate his sled dogs on a strict
schedule, and sledged miles back again without the
slightest touch of frostbite, scurvy, or snow blindness,
though one of his four companions did get a toothache—
don't hold much interest for me. "Of course they don't,"
said George. "You're a romantic. What's romantic about a
guy wanting to go somewhere and *getting* there?"

In the pantheon of British polar failures, no one could
be more romantic than the man Amundsen beat, Captain
Robert Falcon Scott, for whom I have long harbored especially tender feelings. One of the many reasons I own a
dozen books about him is that he and his party were bookish
sorts themselves. One tends to picture polar explorers as unwashed fellows slogging wordlessly through the snow on

half-rations of pemmican hoosh, and so they often were. But before many of those slogs began, the men had to overwinter at surprisingly civilized base camps, of which Cape Evans, the cozy little Antarctic hut where Scott and his twenty-four men spent the winter of 1911, was far and away the most highbrow. Three nights a week after dinner—which on special occasions included seal consommé and stewed penguin breast—Scott convened sessions of what he called the Universitas Antarctica. Topics for discussion included the future of aviation, the art of Japan, and the parasitology of fish. On non-Universitas evenings, the men listened to Caruso on their gramophone, wrote poetry, painted watercolors, or read books from the Odd Shelves some of them had imported 14,000 miles. Scott himself brought a selection of Russian and Polish novels. Captain Lawrence Edward Grace Oates, an Old Etonian who was described by one of the seamen as "a gentleman, quite a gentleman, and always a gentleman," brought all five volumes of Charles James Napier's *Peninsular War*, an epic study of the Napoleonic campaigns in Iberia. Edward Wilson, the chief of the scientific staff—the man who had raised the penguin chick on Scott's previous expedition to Antarctica—brought the works of Tennyson. After reading "In Memoriam," he wrote in his diary that he had "been realising what a perfect piece of faith and hope and religion it is, [and it] makes me feel that if the end comes to me here or hereabout . . . all will be as it is meant to be."

Wilson's diary entry could not have been more prescient.

As any English schoolboy can tell you, Scott, Oates, Wilson, Lieutenant Henry Bowers, and Petty Officer Edgar Evans—slowed by bad weather, inadequate rations, inferior clothing, second-rate tents, and, because they were animal lovers, a masochistic insistence on man-hauling their sledge for most of the journey rather than using dogs—reached the South Pole on January 17, 1912, only to find that Amundsen had planted the Norwegian flag there thirty-four days earlier. On February 17, a month into their return trip, Evans died after a fall. On March 17, Oates, realizing that his frostbitten and gangrenous feet were handicapping the rest of the party, uttered the most famous and gallant words in the history of polar exploration: "I am just going outside and may be some time." Then he stumbled out of the tent into a blizzard, never to be seen again. It was his thirty-second birthday. *Balder the Beautiful is dead, is dead.*

On March 21, with two days' rations left, Scott, Wilson, and Bowers, all of them faint with hunger and ravaged by scurvy, pitched their tent as a raging gale approached. They had walked 740 miles from the Pole. Their base camp was 140 miles away, and One Ton Depot, where an ample supply of food and fuel was cached, was only eleven miles away.

Seven months later, a search party from Cape Evans found the small green canvas tent. Three frozen corpses lay inside, tucked in their reindeer-hide sleeping bags. Next to Scott's body was a sheaf of letters he had written to his wife and to the wives and mothers of his companions, as well as his journal, which, although he wrote it wearing mittens, is legible, if increasingly wavery, right down to the final entry. "We are weak," he noted, "writing is difficult, but for my own sake I do not regret this journey, which has shown that Englishmen can endure hardships, help one another, and meet death with as great a fortitude as ever in the past."

Scott's last journal is indescribably sad. But for reasons I cannot fully explain, I find myself even more affected whenever I read an account of what the search party found on his sledge: thirty-five pounds of rocks containing late-Paleozoic fossil leaves and stems of the genus *Glossopteris*, which the men had dragged 400 miles from the Beardmore Glacier. Scott had been so eager to travel light that he had weighed his party's food rations to the last fraction of an ounce, but he didn't dump the rocks. If he had, he and his men might have been able to walk the last eleven miles.

If I had to name the dearest part of my Odd Shelf, I think it would be the pages that describe those geological specimens. The annals of polar exploration contain many moments of triumph, and even more of farce, but they are also filled with death. The lesson these books have taught me is that if you are going to be a martyr, you had better choose your animus with care. When I think of the causes for which people more commonly give up their lives—nationalism, religion, ethnicity—it seems to me that a thirty-five-pound bag of rocks, and the lost world it represents, is not such a bad thing to die for.

I recently read that William Kunstler, the radical defense attorney, has written sonnets for more than fifty years. A divine afflatus apparently descended on him after the arrest of O. J. Simpson, provoking a verse called "When the Cheering Stopped." This work consists of fourteen lines of iambic pentameter, incorporating allusions to the Heisman Trophy and Hertz Rent-a-Car, and ends with the prosodically unimpeachable couplet "He's learned the cruelest lesson of them all— / Celebrity does not prevent a fall." Kunstler seems untroubled by his tin ear. In re O.J., he asserts, "Of one thing I am certain, this will not be my last sonnet about the matter."

I felt a warm rush of fellow feeling for Mr. Kunstler, because I too have been a writer of bad sonnets. Cleaning out my file cabinets a few weeks ago, I came upon the following example, titled "Interview with a Soldier":

> *Oh sure! I guess I'll cheer like all the rest*
> *When this is through and we can all go back—*

> *Sometimes I think this stuff is like a test*
> *Of nerves, and one more sleepless night, you'll crack.*
> *It's funny—little kids all want to fight,*
> *But later, when you get your card, it's—well—*
> *It's different, not so great. And now, at night,*
> *You tell the world, shut up or go to hell.*
> *A hero's death is fine—I'd hate to crawl*
> *Away to die. You're nuts to think you go*
> *To Hell . . . This Catholic—he prayed and all—*
> *Blown up—I think they found a finger, though.*
> *But Christ! It came damn near me—I'm okay*
> *Though. Nothing happened bad at all that day.*

"Interview with a Soldier" was dated May 21, 1967. I was thirteen. I wrote it for Miss Farrar's ninth-grade English class at the Marlborough School for Girls in Los Angeles. At the time, I knew as much about being a soldier in Vietnam as I knew about sex or politics, two of my other favorite poetic themes, but that didn't stop me. I thought my sonnet was as brutal and sophisticated as anything ever written, a trenchant cross between Siegfried Sassoon and J. D. Salinger, but deserving of extra points for cramming all that nihilism into a mere fourteen lines.

I happened to leave my yellowed copy of "Interview with a Soldier" on the bedside table, where it was spotted by my husband. George and I have few secrets, but during our ten years together I had never shown him any of my poems. This may have something to do with the fact that when George was in his twenties, he was a *real* poet, who published in places like *Ploughshares* and *The Southern Poetry Review*.

"Hmmm," he said, choosing his words carefully. "It scans well."

Sometimes I think that my tombstone will read, "She scanned well." For, alas, George had summed up my essential character in three words. Beneath my sonnet's hard-boiled exterior—it was no mean feat to work in "Hell," "Christ," *and* "damn"—cowered the soul of an unregenerate goody-goody, a priggish little pedant who would no more have permitted a rogue trochee to sneak among her perfect iambs than show up in Miss Farrar's class with a smudge on her monogrammed school uniform.

It was a grievous blow when Miss Farrar tacked up the class's star sonnets on the bulletin board and mine was not among them. Her favorite was about the Acropolis. Twenty-eight years later, I still remember that its author called the Parthenon "a ruined crown." It never occurred to me that this metaphor alone was worth a hundred of my entire sonnet; all I noticed, in my wounded condition, was that my rival's verse *didn't scan*. It was only at sixteen, when I read Shakespeare's Sonnet 116 ("Let me not to the marriage of true minds / Admit impediments. Love is not love . . .") and Hopkins's "The Windhover" ("Brute beauty and valor and act, oh, air, pride, plume, here / Buckle!"), that I realized that these poets had failed to stick to iambic pentameter not because they couldn't but because they didn't want to.

By that time I had written twenty or thirty sonnets, of which—I know this will come as a grave disappointment to future anthologists—only four are extant. In form, they

were all Shakespearean (three quatrains and a couplet)
rather than Petrarchan (an octave and a sestet), because
Shakespearean sonnets, having seven rhymes rather than
only four or five, were easier. (My success-grubbing disposition craved a certain amount of challenge but was loath
to assume an optional handicap that the more philistine
members of my imagined reading public might not even
recognize.) The Fadiman oeuvre was uniformly bleak. One
sonnet written at fifteen, about a seedy section of Holly-
wood Boulevard upon which I had cast my cynical gaze
while waiting in a movie line, ended with the couplet
"While in the movie many people died / I saw more death
while killing time outside." It scanned well.

All this time, like Molière's *bourgeois gentilhomme*, who
congratulated himself for having spoken prose all his life,
I was under the impression that I was writing poetry. My
sonnets looked like poems. They quacked like poems. But
at seventeen, when I got to college and my critical faculties
suddenly kicked in, I had to admit that they weren't really
poems. I had mistaken for lyric genius what was in fact
merely the genetic facility for verbal problem-solving that
enabled everyone in my family to excel at crossword puz-
zles, anagrams, and Scrabble. Since that awful realization,
I haven't written a single poem aside from the doggerel I
trot out at friends' weddings. How I envy Mr. Kunstler for
the suspension of disbelief that has enabled him to carry
on for half a century!

The question remains: During my brief career as a soi-disant poet, why did I restrict myself almost entirely to sonnets? In retrospect, I believe I saw the form as a vindication of both my temperament and my physical self. I was small and compulsive; I was not suited to the epic or to free verse; in work as in life, I was fated to devote myself not to the grand scheme but to the lapidary detail. The sonnet, with its epigrammatic compression and formal structure (never twelve lines, never sixteen), hearteningly proclaimed that smallness and small-mindedness need not go hand in hand. A sonnet might *look* dinky, but it was somehow big enough to accommodate love, war, death, and O. J. Simpson. You could fit the whole world in there if you shoved hard enough.

That was why I was particularly drawn to two Wordsworth sonnets about the sonnet. One was called "Nuns Fret Not at Their Convent's Narrow Room." Its theme is the paradoxically liberating power of restriction. Just as a nun does not feel cramped in her cell because, however tiny, it is roomy enough to admit God, so the poet may find his imagination emancipated by the sonnet's modest compass: "In truth, the prison, into which we doom / Ourselves, no prison is; and hence for me, / In sundry moods, 'twas pastime to be bound / Within the Sonnet's scanty plot of ground."

In the second poem, "Scorn Not the Sonnet," Wordsworth summoned a glorious procession of poets—Shakespeare, Petrarch, Tasso, Camoëns, Dante, Spenser—who, tormented by lost love, exile, or depression, had found con-

solation in the sonnet form. He ended with Milton, who
wrote his greatest sonnets after he went blind in his early
forties: ". . . when a damp / Fell round the path of Milton,
in his hand / The Thing became a trumpet."

T he theme of the sonnet's consolatory power has special
meaning to me because of what happened to my father
two years ago, when he was eighty-eight. Over the period
of a week, he had, for mysterious reasons, gone from being
able to read *The Encyclopaedia Britannica* to being unable
to read the *E* at the top of an eye chart. I took him from
the west coast of Florida, where he and my mother live,
to the Bascom Palmer Eye Institute in Miami. He was
informed there that he had acute retinal necrosis, improb-
ably caused by a chicken-pox virus that had been latent for
more than eighty years. He was unlikely to regain much
of his sight.

I spent the night on a cot in my father's hospital room.
We talked about his life's pleasures and disappointments.
At some point after midnight, he said, "I don't wish to be
melodramatic, but you should know that if I can't read or
write, I'm finished." Never retired, he was accustomed to
working a sixty-hour week as an editor and critic.

"Well, Milton wrote *Paradise Lost* after *he* went blind,"
I said, grasping at straws.

"So he did," said my father. "He also wrote that famous
sonnet."

" 'On His Blindness,' " I replied. I had read it at thirteen, the year I wrote my own first sonnet.

" 'When I consider how my light is spent'—then how does it go?" he said. "Isn't there a preposition next?"

In the darkness, we managed between us to reconstruct six and a half of the fourteen lines. "When you get back to New York," he said, "the first thing I want you to do is to look up that sonnet and read it to me over the telephone."

There was no way to know at the time that over the next year my father would learn to use recorded books, lecture without notes, and gain access to unguessed-at inner resources—in short, to discover that the convent's narrow room that he had been forced to occupy was, though terrible, considerably wider than he had expected. All these things lay far in the future, but that night in Miami, Milton's sonnet provided the first glimmer of the persistent intellectual curiosity that was to prove his saving grace.

When I returned home, I called him at the hospital and read him the sonnet:

> *When I consider how my light is spent*
> *Ere half my days, in this dark world and wide,*
> *And that one talent which is death to hide,*
> *Lodged with me useless, though my soul more bent*
> *To serve therewith my Maker, and present*
> *My true account, lest he returning chide;*
> *"Doth God exact day-labor, light denied?"*
> *I fondly ask; But Patience to prevent*

That murmur, soon replies, "God doth not need
Either man's work or his own gifts; who best
Bear his mild yoke, they serve him best. His state
Is kingly. Thousands at his bidding speed
And post o'er land and ocean without rest:
They also serve who only stand and wait."

"Of course," said my pessimistic, areligious father. "How could I have forgotten?"

When I was eleven and my brother was thirteen, our parents took us to Europe. At the Hôtel d'Angleterre in Copenhagen, as he had done virtually every night of his literate life, Kim left a book facedown on the bedside table. The next afternoon, he returned to find the book closed, a piece of paper inserted to mark the page, and the following note, signed by the chambermaid, resting on its cover:

SIR, YOU MUST NEVER DO THAT TO A BOOK.

My brother was stunned. How could it have come to pass that he—a reader so devoted that he'd sneaked a book and a flashlight under the covers at his boarding school every night after lights-out, a crime punishable by a swat with a wooden paddle—had been branded as *someone who didn't love books*? I shared his mortification. I could not imagine a more bibliolatrous family than the Fadimans. Yet, with the exception of my mother, in the eyes of the

young Danish maid we would all have been found guilty
of rampant book abuse.

During the next thirty years I came to realize that just
as there is more than one way to love a person, so is there
more than one way to love a book. The chambermaid believed in courtly love. A book's physical self was sacrosanct
to her, its form inseparable from its content; her duty as a
lover was Platonic adoration, a noble but doomed attempt
to conserve forever the state of perfect chastity in which it
had left the bookseller. The Fadiman family believed in
carnal love. To us, a book's *words* were holy, but the paper,
cloth, cardboard, glue, thread, and ink that contained them
were a mere vessel, and it was no sacrilege to treat them
as wantonly as desire and pragmatism dictated. Hard use
was a sign not of disrespect but of intimacy.

Hilaire Belloc, a courtly lover, once wrote:

> *Child! do not throw this book about;*
> *Refrain from the unholy pleasure*
> *Of cutting all the pictures out!*
> *Preserve it as your chiefest treasure.*

What would Belloc have thought of my father, who, in
order to reduce the weight of the paperbacks he read on
airplanes, tore off the chapters he had completed and threw
them in the trash? What would he have thought of my
husband, who reads in the sauna, where heat-fissioned
pages drop like petals in a storm? What would he have

thought (here I am making a brazen attempt to upgrade my family by association) of Thomas Jefferson, who chopped up a priceless 1572 first edition of Plutarch's works in Greek in order to interleave its pages with an English translation? Or of my old editor Byron Dobell, who, when he was researching an article on the Grand Tour, once stayed up all night reading six volumes of Boswell's journals and, as he puts it, "sucked them like a giant mongoose"? Byron told me, "I didn't give a damn about the condition of those volumes. In order to get where I had to go, I underlined them, wrote in them, shredded them, dropped them, tore them to pieces, and did things to them that we can't discuss in public."

Byron loves books. Really, he does. So does my husband, an incorrigible book-splayer whose roommate once informed him, "George, if you ever break the spine of one of my books, I want you to know you might as well be breaking *my own spine*." So does Kim, who reports that despite his experience in Copenhagen, his bedside table currently supports three spreadeagled volumes. "They are ready in an instant to let me pick them up," he explains. "To use an electronics analogy, closing a book on a bookmark is like pressing the Stop button, whereas when you leave the book facedown, you've only pressed Pause." I confess to marking my place promiscuously, sometimes splaying, sometimes committing the even more grievous sin of dog-earing the page. (Here I manage to be simultaneously abusive and compulsive: I turn down the upper corner for page-marking and the lower corner to identify passages I want to xerox for my commonplace book.)

All courtly lovers press Stop. My Aunt Carol—who will probably claim she's no relation once she finds out how I treat my books—places reproductions of Audubon paintings horizontally to mark the exact paragraph where she left off. If the colored side is up, she was reading the left-hand page; if it's down, the right-hand page. A college classmate of mine, a lawyer, uses his business cards, spurning his wife's silver Tiffany bookmarks because they are a few microns too thick and might leave vestigial stigmata. Another classmate, an art historian, favors Paris Métro tickets or "those inkjet-printed credit card receipts—but only in books of art criticism whose pretentiousness I wish to desecrate with something really crass and financial. I would never use those in fiction or poetry, which really *are* sacred."

Courtly lovers always remove their bookmarks when the assignation is over; carnal lovers are likely to leave romantic mementos, often three-dimensional and messy. *Birds of Yosemite and the East Slope*, a volume belonging to a science writer friend, harbors an owl feather and the tip of a squirrel's tail, evidence of a crime scene near Tioga Pass. A book critic I know took *The Collected Stories and Poems of Edgar Allan Poe* on a backpacking trip through the Yucatán, and whenever an interesting bug landed in it, she clapped the covers shut. She amassed such a bulging insectarium that she feared Poe might not make it through customs. (He did.)

The most permanent, and thus to the courtly lover the most terrible, thing one can leave in a book is one's own words. Even I would never write in an encyclopedia (except perhaps with a No. 3 pencil, which I'd later erase). But I've been annotating novels and poems—transforming monologues into dialogues—ever since I learned to read. Byron Dobell says that his most beloved books, such as *The Essays of Montaigne*, have been written on so many times, in so many different periods of his life, in so many colors of ink, that they have become palimpsests. I would far rather read Byron's copy of Montaigne than a virginal one from the bookstore, just as I would rather read John Adams's copy of Mary Wollstonecraft's *French Revolution*, in whose margins he argued so vehemently with the dead author ("Heavenly times!" "A barbarous theory." "Did this lady think three months time enough to form a free constitution for twenty-five millions of Frenchmen?") that, two hundred years later, his handwriting still looks angry.

Just think what courtly lovers miss by believing that the only thing they are permitted to do with books is *read* them! What do they use for shims, doorstops, glueing weights, and rug-flatteners? When my friend the art historian was a teenager, his cherished copy of *D'Aulaire's Book of Greek Myths* served as a drum pad on which he practiced percussion riffs from Led Zeppelin. A philosophy professor at my college, whose baby became enamored of the portrait of David Hume on a Penguin paperback, had the cover laminated in plastic so her daughter could cut her teeth on the great thinker. Menelik II, the emperor of

Ethiopia at the turn of the century, liked to chew pages from his Bible. Unfortunately, he died after consuming the complete Book of Kings. I do not consider Menelik's fate an argument for keeping our hands and teeth off our books; the lesson to be drawn, clearly, is that he, too, should have laminated his pages in plastic.

"How beautiful to a genuine lover of reading are the sullied leaves, and worn-out appearance . . . of an old 'Circulating Library' Tom Jones, or Vicar of Wakefield!" wrote Charles Lamb. "How they speak of the thousand thumbs that have turned over their pages with delight! . . . Who would have them a whit less soiled? What better condition could we desire to see them in?" Absolutely none. Thus, a landscape architect I know savors the very smell of the dirt embedded in his botany texts; it is the alluvium of his life's work. Thus, my friend the science writer considers her *Mammals of the World* to have been enhanced by the excremental splotches left by Bertrand Russell, an orphaned band-tailed pigeon who perched on it when he was learning to fly. And thus, even though I own a clear plastic cookbook holder, I never use it. What a pleasure it will be, thirty years hence, to open *The Joy of Cooking* to page 581 and behold part of the *actual egg yolk* that my daughter glopped into her very first batch of blueberry muffins at age twenty-two months! The courtly mode simply doesn't work with small children. I hope I am not deluding myself when I imagine that even the Danish chambermaid, if she is now a mother, might be able to appreciate a really grungy copy of *Pat the Bunny*—a book that *invites* the reader to act like a Dobellian giant mongoose— in which Mummy's ring has been fractured and Daddy's scratchy face has been rubbed as smooth as the Blarney Stone.

The trouble with the carnal approach is that we love our books to pieces. My brother keeps his disintegrating *Golden Guide to Birds* in a Ziploc bag. "It consists of dozens of separate fascicles," says Kim, "and it's impossible to read. When I pick it up, the egrets fall out. But if I replaced it, the note I wrote when I saw my first trumpeter swan wouldn't be there. Also, I don't want to admit that so many species names have changed. If I bought a new edition, I'd feel I was being unfaithful to my old friend the yellow-bellied sapsucker, which has been split into three different species."

My friend Clark's eight thousand books, mostly works of philosophy, will never suffer the same fate as *The Golden Guide to Birds*. In fact, just *hearing* about Kim's book might trigger a nervous collapse. Clark, an investment analyst, won't let his wife raise the blinds until sundown, lest the bindings fade. He buys at least two copies of his favorite books, so that only one need be subjected to the stress of having its pages turned. When his visiting mother-in-law made the mistake of taking a book off the shelf, Clark shadowed her around the apartment to make sure she didn't do anything unspeakable to it—such as placing it facedown on a table.

I know these facts about Clark because when George was over there last week, he talked to Clark's wife and made some notes on the back flyleaf of Herman Wouk's *Don't Stop the Carnival*, which he happened to be carrying in his backpack. He ripped out the page and gave it to me.

Six years ago, the week my first child was born, my mother sent me a book that had once belonged to my great-grandmother. The timing was coincidental. My parents were about to move from California to Florida and were divesting themselves of everything that wouldn't fit in their new, smaller house. Because I had been allotted the silver candlesticks, the mother-of-pearl fish knives, and the cut-glass pickle dish, my mother threw in the book, which she had never read, because it, too, was decorative and ancestral.

The book was called *The Mirror of True Womanhood: A Book of Instruction for Women in the World*. The binding was umber, with an ornate design of flowers and leaves embossed on the cover. The pages were edged with gilt. When I grazed my fingernail down the title page, I could feel the letterpress indentations. The bottom of the spine was ragged, evidence that it had been frequently teased off a high shelf with a crooked finger.

Inside the front cover was a bookplate from St. Mary's Academy in Salt Lake City. Five lines of microscopic Spencerian script—the upstrokes were as fine as a baby's hair —reported that the book had been awarded to Miss Maude Earll on June 21, 1886, for excellence in "Arithmetic, Algebra, Geometry, Trigonometry, Grammar, Rhetoric, M. Philosophy, Logic, Botany, Literature, G. History, Penmanship, Astronomy, Elocution, Comp. and L. Writing, Plain Sewing, Ornamental Needlework, Guitar & Bookkeeping."

My great-grandmother Maude has always been considered an exotic character in my family because in our denominational hotchpotch—I'm descended from Jews, Presbyterians, Episcopalians, Mormons, and a Christian Scientist—she was the only Catholic. Her Protestant parents had sent her to a convent school on the condition that the Sisters of the Holy Cross never attempt to convert her. The nuns must have valued Maude's soul more highly than their promise, for she was a devout believer by the time she graduated. The prize they chose for her is the only book I own that belonged to a great-grandparent, or even a grandparent. When my mother sent it to me, all I knew about Maude was that she had knee-length auburn hair, so heavy it gave her headaches, which she eventually cut off and sold for twenty-five dollars, the same price Jo got for hers in *Little Women*; that she had refined manners; and that she could sew stitches so fine they were invisible.

I first read *The Mirror of True Womanhood* while nursing my daughter in a rocking chair, in the midst of the tumult, part ecstasy and part panic, into which all first-time mothers are thrown by sleep deprivation and head-long identity realignment. The book appalled me. It belonged to that hoary genre of women's advice manuals —it shares a call number at the Library of Congress with such descendants as *Having It All*; *Strategy in the Sex War*; and *Help for the Hassled, Hurried, and Hustled*—which, in 1877, when it was published, were almost invariably written by men. The author was the Reverend Bernard O'Reilly, a New York priest who had been chaplain of the Irish Brigade of the Army of the Potomac during the Civil War. Into twenty-two hortatory chapters ("The True Woman's Kingdom: The Home"; "The Wife's Crowning Duty: Fidelity"; "The Mother's Office Toward Boyhood and Girlhood"), Father O'Reilly managed to stuff everything he thought a woman should know. This was the bottom line: "Woman's entire existence, in order to be a source of happiness to others as well as to herself, must be one of self-sacrifice." If she toed the mark, her home would become "the sweetest, brightest, dearest spot of earth." If she transgressed, she might end up like the selfish mother, en route to Europe, whose vessel was "wrecked amid the icebergs off the coast of Newfoundland," or the lazy housewife who suffered the even more dire fate of having her disappointed husband "migrate to California." *Father O'Reilly!* I would mentally chide the author, as I rocked my daughter. *You never had a wife! You never had children!*

How dare you tell my great-grandmother how to lead her life? How dare you tell ME?

Father O'Reilly was damnably sure of himself, or maybe it just seemed that way because, at the time, I was so unsure of myself. I mocked his Victorian priggery, but I was secretly afraid that he was right about motherhood— that, in fact, my id was about to be permanently squashed by my superego. I was working at home as a writer; for the first time, George was the principal breadwinner. "Men are born to be the providers in the home: they are formed by nature and still further fitted by education for every species of toil," I read. "Theirs is the battle of life on sea and land. The home with its quiet, its obscurity, its sanctities, is for woman: she is made to grow up in the shade." What if I got stuck in that shade and never managed to crawl back out?

Of course Father O'Reilly called us "the weaker sex," but I got the feeling he was just bluffing. His heroines nurtured their children with enough motherlove to suffocate a small army. They ministered to lepers, adopted disfigured orphans, and brought bread to poor families "during the most inclement winter's weather." His men were sad sacks by comparison, forever courting disaster either through their own weakness (intemperance, adultery, dimwitted investments) or through rotten luck (maimed hands, amputated legs, paralytic rheumatism). But the wives unfalteringly stood by their men, coaxing them out of their vicious habits and compensating for their infir-

mities by working ever harder themselves. My favorite
O'Reilly anecdote involved a particularly churlish husband:

> Coming home one day at his dinner hour, and finding that
> the meal was not ready, he flew into a furious passion, and
> began to upset and break the furniture in the dining-room.
> His wife—a holy woman—endeavored to pacify him, and,
> while urging the servants to hurry forward their preparations,
> she argued sweetly with her husband on the unseemliness of
> such displays of anger, and begged him to read a book, while
> she would go to aid the cook. He flung the book away from
> him, and stalked back and forth in a rage, while the lady
> hastened to her kitchen.

After a while, chastened by his wife's example (and perhaps by the eventual arrival of dinner), the husband picked
up the book and began to read. By an amazing stroke of
luck, it happened to be *The Lives of the Saints*. The husband reformed his character on the spot and "added one
more name to the long roll of Christian heroes, who owed,
under Providence, their greatness and heroism to the irresistible influence of a saintly woman."

I've got your number, Father O'Reilly, I thought. *It's the
old pedestal trick. We're better than men, so we don't need
to be equal to them.* Of course, a little pedestal deployment
wouldn't *entirely* spoil my day. Once, looking up from a
passage on the ideal wife, I asked George, "Do you consider
me a peerless flower of beauty and spotless purity which

has been laid upon your bosom?" George responded with a neutral, peace-preserving, but not quite affirmative grunt.

Five months ago, after our second child was born, I picked up *The Mirror of True Womanhood* again. It seemed to go with nursing a baby. This time I felt far more confident —motherhood had, in fact, turned out to be a source of joy that had shanghaied neither my brain nor my id—and, perhaps as a result, Father O'Reilly seemed far less confident. His sacralization of the hearth no longer seemed smug; it seemed anxious. In 1877, he could feel the ground shifting beneath his feet. The "home sanctuary" seemed to him the last bulwark against irreligion, evolutionism, crime, alcoholism, prostitution, political corruption, industrial labor, disrespect for the older generation, and female emancipation. "Close and bar the door of your home at all times," he cautioned, "when you know that wickedness is abroad in the street or on the highway." *It's okay, Father O'Reilly*, I told him. *There are lots of people today who feel exactly the same way.*

This time around, the prescribed distaff virtues didn't sound so awful. (In fact, I decided that if they were compulsory for men as well, the world would be a kinder and gentler place.) One night I compiled a brief O'Reilly list and asked George to rate me on a ten-point scale. Here's how I stacked up:

Discretion	7
Discipline	5
Religious fervor	0
Power to soothe and charm	6
Truthfulness	10
Thrift	3
Avoidance of impure literature, engravings, paintings, and statuary	2
Kindness	10
Cheerfulness	6
Order in the Home	5
Abjuration of fashion	10
Self-control	9
Excellence in needlework	2

My scores wouldn't have earned me a prize book from the Sisters of the Holy Cross, but I confess to a small, retrograde flush of pride at not having utterly flunked.

After the second reading, I started asking my mother and my aunt about the woman who had won it. I learned that Maude's husband, Joseph Sharp, a wealthy young man who had studied the classics at Harvard, was superintendent of the coal mine in Sunnyside, Utah, a position that placed him at the top of the local social ladder. His beautiful wife was a renowned hostess until Joseph quit his job over a matter of principle. My mother remembers that there was an explosion in the mine, and the mine owners forbade him to open the doors to let the trapped miners escape, lest the oxygen spread the fire. My aunt remembers that there was a labor strike, and that the owners turned the miners' families out of the company houses in mid-winter, forcing them to live in holes they dug in the snow. Whatever the reason, Joseph and Maude moved without servants to a dairy ranch, where the winner of the trigonometry and elocution prizes scrubbed laundry on a washboard, killed mice by smashing them with a coal shovel, and rose before dawn to bake bread for a kitchenful of ranch hands wearing unwashed longjohns.

When their farmhouse burned to the ground, they lost all they owned except a few things, including Maude's prize book, which she had given to their daughter. Unable to afford rebuilding, they hauled a four-room miner's shack to the ranch on a horse-drawn wagon. It was unpainted and uninsulated. There were no pictures on the walls, no rugs on the floor, no gewgaws on the mantel, no mantel. Maude slept on a plain metal cot whose legs rested in cans filled with bedbug-deterrent turpentine.

In a subchapter called "How a Noble Husband Was Sustained by a Devoted Wife While Passing Through Financial Difficulties," Father O'Reilly told the story of a rich man who suffered a reversal of fortune. His "proud little housewife" offered to sell some of their furniture, saying, "You shall see how easy it will be to me to part with thy treasures, provided I have a little home for you and our darlings." The family, accompanied by their servants, cheerfully set themselves up again in a more modest house. "The carpets were plain, it is true, and the furniture was of the commonest kind; but chairs and sofas and ottomans had been covered with a chintz so pretty that no one stopped to inquire what was beneath the covering. . . . The little ones saw no change around them, save that the light of their mother's smile was even more sunny than ever."

Maude must have read this. Did she want to smash its author with a coal shovel for suggesting that reduced circumstances meant asking your servants to plump chintz-covered cushions insted of satin ones? (I would have. I didn't really deserve that 9 in Self-control.) Or was she in some way consoled?

Father O'Reilly, I think as I sit with my baby on one knee and a worn brown volume on the other, *you and I don't exactly see eye to eye. But thanks for letting me get to know my great-grandmother.* And I tell him that someday I'll ask my daughter what she sees reflected when *she* looks into *The Mirror of True Womanhood.* She'll have plenty to go on, since she'll inherit her great-great-grandmother's book the week her first child is born.

Long ago, when George and I were not yet lovers but seemed to be tottering in that general direction, we gave each other our first Christmas presents. Of course, they were books. Knowing that I liked bears, George gave me *The Biography of a Grizzly*, by Ernest Thompson Seton. Modestly sequestered on the third page was the following inscription: *To a new true friend.* No Talmudic scholar, no wartime cryptographer, no deconstructionist critic ever scrutinized a text more closely than I did those five words, hoping that if they were just construed with the right emphasis ("To a *new* true friend." "To a new *true* friend." "To a new true *friend*"), they would suddenly reveal themselves as a declaration of undying devotion.

Knowing that George liked fish, I gave him *Old Mr. Flood*, by Joseph Mitchell, a slim volume of stories about the Fulton Fish Market. The author had autographed the book himself in 1948, but did I leave well enough alone? Of course not. I wrote: *To George, with love from Anne.*

Then I mistranscribed a quotation from Red Smith. And finally—on the principle that if you don't know what to say, say everything—I added fifteen lines of my own reflections on the nature of intimacy. My cumulative verbiage, not to mention the patency of my sentiments, exceeded George's by a factor of approximately twenty to one. It's a miracle that the book, its recipient, and the new true friendship weren't all crushed under the weight of the inscription.

Unfortunately—since George married me anyway and has retained his affection for both fish and Joseph Mitchell—my words were preserved for good. Unlike the card that accompanies, say, a sweater, from which it is soon likely to part company, a book and its inscription are permanently wedded. This can be either a boon or a blot. As Seumas Stewart, the proprietor of an antiquarian bookshop in Chipping Campden, Gloucestershire, has observed, "Imagine how delightful it would be to own an edition of Thomson's *The Seasons* with this authenticated inscription: *To my dear friend John Keats in admiration and gratitude, from P. B. Shelley, Florence, 1820.* Imagine, too, how depressing to have an otherwise fine first of Milton's *Paradise Lost* with this ball-point inscription scrawled on the title page: *To Ada from Jess, with lots of love and candy floss, in memory of a happy holiday at Blackpool, 1968.*"

My inscription, a specimen of the candy-floss school, did not improve *Old Mr. Flood* in the same way that, for example, *To Miss Elizabeth Barrett with the Respects of Ed-*

gar Allan Poe improved *The Raven and Other Poems*, or *Hans Christian Andersen / From his friend and admirer Charles Dickens / London July 1847* improved *The Pickwick Papers*. In the bibliomane's hierarchy, such holy relics of literary tangency eclipse all other factors: binding, edition, rarity, condition. "The meanest, most draggle-tailed, foxed, flead, dog's-eared drab of a volume" (as the critic and bibliophile Holbrook Jackson once wrote) is instantly transfigured by an inscription with a sufficiently distinguished pedigree. Whose hands could fail to tremble while holding the well-worn copy of *Corinne*, by Madame de Staël, on whose flyleaf Byron wrote a 226-word mash note to the Marchesa Guiccioli that ends, *I more than love you, and cannot cease to love you. Think of me sometimes when the Alps and the ocean divide us,—but they never will, unless you wish it.* (Now *that's* the sort of thing I wouldn't have minded finding inside *The Biography of a Grizzly*.)

Even in the heat of passion, Byron remembered to observe proper inscription etiquette by writing on the flyleaf instead of the title page, which is traditionally reserved for a book's author. I learned this only recently, after having defaced dozens of other writers' title pages. I should have cracked the code years ago, since the Books by Friends and Relatives section of our own library contains a profusion of title-page inscriptions, all licitly deployed. My father inscribed *Famous Monster Tales*, an anthology to which he contributed a preface when I was a sullen fourteen-year-old, *For Anne, from that old monster, Daddy*. Mark Helprin, who likes to leave messages on his friends' answering machines in spurious (but highly convincing) dialects, inscribed several of his books in imaginary languages. In *A Dove of the East*, he wrote *Skanaarela tan floss atcha atcha qumble ta. Da bubo barta flay? Staarcroft.* I spent the better part of a decade trying in vain to figure out what that meant.

A distant rung down from the "presentation copy"—an inscribed book actually presented by the author as a gift —is the "inscription copy," a book inscribed (sometimes, one suspects, with a gun to the author's head) at the owner's request. Before the advent of store-sponsored book signings, most readers got a book inscribed by mailing it to the author and praying that it would make a round-trip. Yeats once asked Thomas Hardy how he handled these requests. Hardy led Yeats upstairs to a large room that was filled from floor to ceiling with books—thousands of them. "Yeats," said Hardy, "these are the books that were sent to me for signature."

The first edition of *On Forsyte 'Change* that I saw last month in a secondhand bookstore had obviously made a more fruitful circuit. On the title page, in small, formal handwriting—the work of an old-fashioned fountain pen —were the words *Inscribed for C. F. Sack cordially by John Galsworthy, Oct 6 1930.* Presumably, Galsworthy didn't know C. F. Sack from Adam, and he didn't pretend to. But what are we to make of *To Owen—Love + Kisses—Brooke Shields XX* (to quote from the title page of *On Your Own*, glimpsed in another bookstore)? I feel certain that Ms. Shields had no more intention of kissing Owen than Galsworthy had of kissing C. F. Sack—the fact that she signed her full name is a dead giveaway—but that was no deterrent. Her panting communication, written in black felt-tip pen, filled nearly half the page. (I can report, after a close study of the celebrity-autograph department of the Strand Bookstore in New York City, that the felt-tip pen has achieved near-total hegemony. Barbara Cartland writes in pink, Ivana Trump in purple, and Francine du Plessix Gray in green.)

My friend Mark O'Donnell, whom I consider the nonesuch of inscribers, would never stoop to such tactics. At a signing party for his collection *Vertigo Park and Other Tall Tales*, he came up with something different for each postulant: *Dear Reader, I love you* (an ironic homage to the Shields genre); *No time to write—Life in dang———*; and, the most heartfelt of all, *Thank you for shopping retail.*

Maggie Hivnor, the paperback editor of the University of Chicago Press, once told me that when she adds an out-of-print title to her list, she calls the author and asks for a pristine copy that can be photographically reproduced. "The author is usually a man," she explained. "In a few weeks, a beautifully kept copy of his book arrives, a little dusty perhaps but otherwise absolutely perfect. And on the title page it invariably says *To Mother.*"

Now *that's* a real inscription. The best thing about it is that until the editor's call, the book that it ennobled reposed precisely where it should have: in a place of honor on Mother's shelf. And there it shall return. How melancholy, by contrast, are the legions of inscribed copies one finds in any used-book rack, each a memorial to a betrayed friendship. Do the traitors believe that their faithlessness will remain secret? If so, they are sadly deluded. Hundreds of people will witness it, including, on occasion, the inscriber. Shaw once came across one of his books in a secondhand shop, inscribed *To ——— with esteem, George Bernard Shaw*. He bought the book and returned it to ———, adding the line, *With renewed esteem, George Bernard Shaw*.

I once saw a copy of *Mayflower Madam* inscribed by Sydney Biddle Barrows *To Patrick—Richard has told me so much about you.* Henry Miller could have written an entire novel about that inscription. It would take Turgenev to write a novel about the inscription I found in *The Golden Book: The Story of Fine Books and Bookmaking.* It read: *To Father on his birthday, March 16, 1928. In the nature of a peace offering? Alan.* After sixty-seven years, that heartbreaking question mark still hangs in the air. I only hope that *The Golden Book* found its way to a bookseller long after Father's death. If not, Father, shame on you.

Fortunately, the very finest inscriptions, like the finest love letters, rarely pass out of a family. The most bravura performance I've seen—testimony that the art of the romantic inscription was not buried with Byron—graces the Oxford Classical Text of the complete works of Virgil, given to my friend Maud Gleason when she was reading *litterae humaniores* at Oxford. Maud says she would no sooner part with it than with her son's first tooth. As she explained to me, "I had repaired to the King's Arms, the pub closest to the Bodleian Library, with a fellow student, a dashing but bullheaded young Scotsman who proclaimed over coffee that Homer was vastly inferior to Virgil. As a Homeric partisan, I was much miffed, even though, as the conversation progressed, I had to confess that I had never actually *read* Virgil. 'If you think Virgil's so great,' said I, the brash American, 'why don't you give me a copy?' Soon thereafter a blue volume arrived on my doorstep, inscribed on the flyleaf with thirteen lines of Latin dactylic hexameter—Virgil's preferred meter." The inscription began *Poscimur; atque aliquid quando tu, cara, requiris / Dabitur* (I am entreated, and when you, dear, ask anything of me, it shall be given); continued with an apostrophe to Maud, whom the Scotsman declared that he admired, as all poets were wont to admire Virgil, *quanto desiderat astra / Papilio volitans* (as the fluttering butterfly longs for the stars); and ended with a pledge *amoris amicitiaeque* (of love and friendship).

"So what happened?" I asked Maud, who now teaches classics at Stanford.

"I never slept with the boy," she said. "But I fell for Virgil, and I've slept with the book many times."

The best inscription *I've* ever gotten—it may not be as

dazzling as the Scotsman's, but I wouldn't trade—is on the title page of *The Enigma of Suicide*, by George Howe Colt. I've never slept with the book, but I've slept with the author many times. It reads (how far we have come, George, since our new true friendship!) *To my beloved wife. . . . This is your book, too. As my life, too, is also yours.*

On November 12, 1838, Thomas Babington Macaulay set out by horse-drawn coach from Florence to Rome. "My journey lay over the field of Thrasymenus," he wrote in his journal, "and as soon as the sun rose, I read Livy's description of the scene."

The moment I read that sentence, I knew that Macaulay and I were peas in a pod. It is true that I had never re-formed the Indian educational system, served in the House of Commons, or written a five-volume history of England, but those were paltry details. He would surely have agreed that we were alike where it really counted: we were both hard-core devotees of what I call You-Are-There Reading, the practice of reading books in the places they describe.

The discovery of our mutual passion was particularly gratifying because Macaulay was probably the greatest reader of all time. He started reading at the age of three, died at fifty-nine with an open book in front of him, and in between, as his nephew observed, read books "faster than other people skimmed them, and skimmed them as fast as any one else could turn the leaves." He particularly liked to read while in transit. He read Bulwer-Lytton's *Alice* while walking across the Pontine Marshes, Plato while rambling on the heath at Tunbridge Wells, and innumerable books while zigzagging rapidly, and apparently without collision, through the crowded streets of London. While sailing to India he read Homer, Virgil, Caesar, Horace, Dante, Petrarch, Ariosto, Tasso, Bacon, Cervantes, and all seventy volumes of Voltaire. That's a partial list. "What a blessing it is to love books as I love them," he wrote to a friend, "to be able to converse with the dead, and to live amidst the unreal!"

When he read Livy at Thrasymenus—in Latin, of course—Macaulay achieved a kind of Double Word Score whose peculiar frisson will be instantly recognized by anyone who has ever read Wordsworth at Grasmere, Gibbon in Rome, or Thoreau at Walden. Thrasymenus, a lake in eastern Etruria, was the site of one of the worst disasters in Roman military history. In 217 B.C., Hannibal, riding the sole survivor of the thirty-eight elephants that had set out across the Alps the previous year, defeated the Roman legions, led by the consul Gaius Flaminius, in the second major battle of the Second Punic War. It was a classic ambush. While marching at dawn through a narrow defile with steep hills on one side and the lake on the other, the Romans were charged simultaneously from the front, the rear, and the left flank by torrents of Carthaginian infantrymen who had been concealed by a dense, low-lying fog.

The Romans who weren't hacked to pieces ended up in the lake, where many of them drowned under the weight of their armor. In three hours, 15,000 Romans died.

When I looked up Livy's description of the battle—it's in book XXII of his history of Rome, which he wrote about two hundred years after Flaminius's defeat—I anticipated dry fare. Well. By the fifth page I was on the edge of my seat; by the tenth my heart rate had palpably accelerated. And that was reading *in my living room.* I had forgotten how incredibly gory, stirring, and intimate combat was before the invention of firearms, when in order to kill your enemy you had to be close enough to stab him with your sword or pierce him with your javelin. "The fog was so thick that ears were of more use than eyes," wrote Livy,

> and the groans of the wounded, the sound of blows on body or armour and the mingled shouts and screams of assailants and assailed made [the Romans] turn and gaze, now this way and now that. . . . When it became apparent that their only hope of safety lay in their right arms and their swords, then every man became his own commander and urged himself to action. . . . And such was the frenzy of their eagerness and so absorbed were they in fighting, that an earthquake, violent enough to overthrow large portions of many of the towns of Italy, turn swift streams from their courses, carry the sea up into rivers, and bring down mountains with great landslides, was not even felt by any of the combatants.

Two thousand and fifty-five years later, Macaulay wrote, "I was exactly in the situation of the consul, Flaminius— completely hid in the morning fog. . . . So that I can truly say that I have seen precisely what the Roman army saw on that day." He had arrived at Thrasymenus not only at the same hour as the original battle but in the same weather! When his coach reached the hilltop, above the fog, he, like Hannibal, had a clear view of the scene. "I then understood the immense advantage which Hannibal derived from keeping his divisions on the heights, where he could see them all, and where they could all see each other, while the Romans were stumbling and groping, without the possibility of concert, through the thick haze below." *Haec est nobilis ad Trasumennum pugna.* Such was the famous battle of Thrasymenus. Such was Macaulay's conversation with the dead.

What makes You-Are-There Reading so much more thrilling to us buffs than You-Are-Somewhere-Else Reading? I think it's because the mind's eye isn't literal enough for us. We want to walk into the pages, the way Woody Allen's Professor Kugelmass walked into *Madame Bovary*, triggering a flurry of scholarly confusion about the bald New Yorker in a leisure suit who had suddenly appeared on page 100. Failing that, the nearest we can come to Macaulay's living "amidst the unreal" is to walk into a book's physical setting. The closer we get, the better. For example, reading Steinbeck in Monterey won't do; we must read him on Cannery Row. Even that backdrop falls short of perfection, for Cannery Row has changed more in a half century than Thrasymenus had in two millennia, and the details on the page no longer match the details before our eyes. The consummate You-Are-There experience requires us, like Macaulay, to see *exactly* what the author described, so that all we need do to cross the eidetic threshold is squint a little.

I've never equaled the sensory verisimilitude of my friend Adam, who once read the ninth book of the *Odyssey*, in Greek, in what is believed to be the Cyclops's cave, a Sicilian grotto Homerically redolent of sheep turds. But I have read Yeats in Sligo, Isak Dinesen in Kenya, and John Muir in the Sierras. By far my finest You-Are-There hour, however, was spent reading the journals of John Wesley Powell, the one-armed Civil War veteran who led the first expedition down the Colorado River, while I was camped at Granite Rapids in the bottom of the Grand Canyon.

In one crucial aspect, I bested Macaulay. Alone on his grand tour, he had no one with whom to share the rapture of Thrasymenus except the shade of Livy. In the Grand Canyon, I had George. It was our first vacation together, and it was full of revelations: that George was afraid of mice; that I never went backpacking without my baby pillow; that we both loved skinny-dipping in water so cold it gave us headaches.

Alone on a beach of almost Caribbean whiteness, walled in by cliffs of black schist and pink granite, George and I had washed each other's hair in the Colorado River and then settled ourselves next to the churning rapids with *The*

Exploration of the Colorado River and Its Canyons.
"G. reads from Powell," I wrote by candlelight in my journal that night, "holding the book on his bare legs. Amazing
to hear of Powell's equipment and food and how hard it
was for him to run the rapids, with the rapids *right in front
of us*!!" There was an engraving of Granite Rapids in the
book. Nothing had changed.

"We are now ready to start on our way down the Great
Unknown," read George. "Our boats, tied to a common
stake, chafe each other as they are tossed by the fretful
river. . . . We have an unknown distance yet to run, an
unknown river to explore. What falls there are, we know
not; what rocks beset the channel, we know not; what walls
rise over the river, we know not." We had no idea at the
time that these are among the most famous sentences in
expedition literature. We thought we had discovered them.
I am grateful for our innocence, just as I am grateful that
I didn't know then that Powell's journals were hashed together from the skimpy notes he scrawled on strips of
brown paper during the expedition, overlaid with impres-
sions from a second trip two years later, further overlaid
with two sets of revisions.

In a voice that could barely be heard above the roar of
the whitewater, George read of spinning in whirlpools,
bashing against rocks, capsizing in waterfalls, losing food
and oars and guns and barometers and blankets and an
entire boat. In the worst stretches, including the rapids at
our feet, Powell couldn't turn right, couldn't turn left,

couldn't slow down, couldn't get out, couldn't do anything but hold on to a leather strap he had fastened to the gunwale and ride his leaky dory like a bucking bronco. Years later, when I read Livy, I was struck by how much Powell's adrenaline-soaked confusion resembled that of the soldiers trapped in the defile at Thrasymenus. Caroming through Granite Rapids, no one would have noticed an earthquake either.

"It is especially cold in the rain to-night," read George. "The little canvas we have is rotten and useless; the rubber *ponchos* with which we started from Green River City have all been lost; more than half the party are without hats, not one of us has an entire suit of clothes, and we have not a blanket apiece. . . . We sit up all night on the rocks, shivering." That was the night of August 17, 1869. Powell and his men had just run Granite Rapids. As the sun set beneath the South Rim, George and I snuggled in polypropylene and Gore-Tex. "For us, only the illusion of peril and discovery," I wrote. "For Powell, the real thing."

That's the catch: it's always the illusion, never the real thing. Or so I thought until last year. George and I have two children now, and our adventures are closer to home. When our daughter was four, she took her copy of *Eloise* to tea at the Plaza Hotel. Macaulay never fought at Thrasymenus. I never ran the Colorado River. But Susannah has *actually* hidden behind the red velvet curtains in the

Grand Ballroom, slomped down the hallway on the fif-
teenth floor, and gotten dizzy in the revolving door with
the ¶P on it. When we got to the Palm Court, Susannah
opened her book to page 40. Her eyes skittered back and
forth between the plate of Gugelhopfen on the triple-tiered
table in the picture and the plate of Gugelhopfen on the
triple-tiered table in front of her. She didn't say a word. I
knew what she was thinking. She was there.

When I was nineteen, William Shawn interviewed me for a summer job at *The New Yorker*. To grasp the full import of what follows, you should know that I considered *The New Yorker* a cathedral and Mr. Shawn a figure so godlike that I expected a faint nimbus to emanate from his ruddy head. During the course of our conversation, he asked me what other magazines I hoped to write for.

"Um, *Esquire*, the *Saturday Review*, and——"

I wanted to say *"Ms.,"* but my lips had already butted against the *M*—too late for a politic retreat—when I realized I had no idea how to pronounce it. Lest you conclude that I had been raised in Ulan Bator, I might remind you that in 1973, when I met Mr. Shawn, *Ms.* magazine had been published for scarcely a year, and most people, including me, had never heard the word *Ms.* used as a term of address. (Mr. Shawn had called me Miss Fadiman. *He* was so venerated by his writers that "Mister" had virtually become part of his name.) Its pronunciation, reflexive now, was not as obvious as you might think. After all, *Mr.* is not pronounced "Mir," and *Mrs.* is not pronounced "Mirz." Was it "Mzzzzz"? "Miz"? "Muz"?

In that apocalyptic split second, I somehow alighted on "Em Ess," which I knew to be the correct pronunciation of *ms.*, or manuscript.

Mr. Shawn didn't blink. He gave no indication that I had said anything untoward. In fact, he calmly proceeded to discuss the new feminist magazine—its history, its merits, its demerits, the opportunities it might offer a young writer like me—for four or five minutes *without ever mentioning its name.*

Since that time, whenever I have heard anyone talk about civility, I have thought of Mr. Shawn, a man so civil that, in order to spare me embarrassment, he succeeded in crossing an entire minefield of potential *Ms.*'s without detonating a single one. I consider his feat comparable to that of Georges Perec, the experimental French writer who composed a 311-page novel without using the letter *e.* After I left the building, I called a friend. ("How do you say that new little word? . . . Oh my God, no!") That was a terrible moment, but as Mr. Shawn had surmised, wanting to die in a telephone booth was greatly preferable to wanting to die in his office.

In twenty-three years—an eyeblink in our linguistic history—the new little word has evolved from a cryptic buzz to an automatism. From the beginning, I saw its logic and fairness. Why should people instantly know if a woman, but not a man, was married? Why should they care? The need for *Ms.* was indisputable. The hitch was feeling comfortable *saying* it. It sounded too much like a lawn mower. Gradually, my ear retuned. Now, although it's probably a moot point—everyone except telephone solicitors calls me Anne—I am, by process of elimination, Ms. Fadiman. I can't be Miss Fadiman because I'm married. I can't be Mrs. Fadiman because my husband is Mr. Colt. I can't be Mrs. Colt because my name is still Fadiman. I am, to my surprise, the very woman for whom *Ms.* was invented.

On the sanguinary fields of gender politics, *Ms.* has scored a clear victory. I wish I could say the same of, say, the United Church of Christ's new "inclusive" hymnal, in which "Dear Lord and Father of Mankind" has been replaced by "Dear God, Embracing Humankind." The end is estimable; it's the means that chafe. I'm not sure I want to be embraced by an Almighty with so little feeling for poetry. Yet, having heard the new version, I can't say I feel entirely happy with the old one either. As is all too often the case these days, I find my peace as a reader and writer rent by a war between two opposing semantic selves, one feminist and one reactionary. Most people who have written about questions of gender bias in language have belonged to one camp or the other. Either they want to change everything, or they don't see what all the fuss is about. Am I the only one who feels torn?

Verbally speaking, as in other areas, my feminist self was born of a simple desire for parity. The use of gender-neutral terms like *flight attendant*, *firefighter*, and *police officer* seems to me an unambiguous step forward, part of the same process that has euthanized such terminal patients as *authoress* and *sculptress*—good riddance!—and is even now working on the gaggingly adorable *-ette* words: usherettes are being promoted to *ushers*, *suffragettes* to *suffragists*. (I have been particularly sensitive to words that make women sound little and cute ever since the day my college roommates and I sat around discussing which animals we all resembled. I'd hoped for something majestic—an eland, perhaps, or a great horned owl—but was unanimously declared a gopher. Given that history, it's a wonder no one has ever called me an authorette.)

My reactionary self, however, prevails when I hear someone attempt to purge the bias from "to each his own" by substituting "to each their own." The disagreement between pronoun and antecedent is more than I can bear. To understand how I feel about grammar, you need to remember that I come from the sort of family in which, at the age of ten, I was told I must always say *hoi polloi*, never "the *hoi polloi*," because *hoi* meant "the," and two "the's" were redundant—indeed something only hoi polloi would say. (Why any ten-year-old would say *hoi polloi* in the first place is another, more pathological matter, but we won't go into that here.)

I call the "to each his own" quandary the His'er Problem, after a solution originally proposed by Chicago school superintendent Ella Young in 1912: "To each his'er own."

I'm sorry. I just can't. My reactionary self has aesthetic as well as grammatical standards, and *his'er* is hideous. Unlike *Ms.*, *his'er* could never become reflexive. (I might interject here that when I posed the His'er Problem to my brother, who was raised in the same grammatical hothouse as I, he surprised me by saying, "I won't say *his'er*. That would be a capitulation to barbarism. But I would be willing to consider a more rhythmically acceptable neologism such as *hyr* or *hes*, which would be preferable to having to avoid *his* by plotting each sentence in advance like a military campaign." My brother clearly doesn't warm to the same challenges as Messrs. Shawn and Perec.)

What about "to each his or her own"? I do resort to that construction occasionally, but I find the double pronoun an ungainly burden. More frequently I recast the entire sentence in the plural, although "to all their own" is slightly off pitch. Even a phrase that is not stylistically disfigured —for example, "all writers worth their salt," which is only marginally more lumpish than "every writer worth his salt"—loses its specificity, that fleeting moment in which the reader conjures up an individual writer (Isaiah Berlin in one mind's eye, Robert James Waller in another) instead of a faceless throng.

But I can't go back. I said "to each his own" until about five years ago, believing what my sixth-grade grammar textbook, *Easy English Exercises*, had told me: that "or her" was "understood," just as womankind was understood to be lurking somewhere within "mankind." I no longer understand. The other day I came across the following sentence by my beloved role model, E. B. White: "There is one thing the essayist cannot do—he cannot indulge himself in deceit or concealment, for he will be found out in no time." I felt the door slamming in my face so fast I could feel the wind against my cheek. "But he *meant* to include you!" some of you may be murmuring. "It was understood!"

I don't think so. Long ago, my father wrote something similar: "The best essays [do not] develop original themes. They develop original men, their composers." Since my father, unlike E. B. White, is still around to testify, I called him up last night and said, "Be honest. What was really in your mind when you wrote those sentences?" He replied, "Males. I was thinking about males. I viewed the world of literature—indeed, the entire world of artistic creation—as a world of males, and so did most writers. Any writer of fifty years ago who denies that is lying. Any male writer, I mean."

I believe that although my father and E. B. White were not misogynists, they didn't really *see* women, and their language reflected and reinforced that blind spot. Our invisibility was brought home to me fifteen years ago, after *Thunder Out of China*, a 1946 best-seller about China's role in the Second World War, was reissued in paperback. Its co-authors were Theodore H. White and Annalee Jacoby, my mother. In his foreword to the new edition, Harrison Salisbury mentioned White nineteen times and my mother

once. His first sentence was "There is, in the end, no substitute for the right man in the right place at the right
moment." I wrote to Salisbury, suggesting that sometimes
—for example, in half of *Thunder Out of China*—there is
no substitute for the right woman in the right place at the
right moment. To his credit, he responded with the following mea culpa: "Oh, oh, oh! You are totally right. I am
entirely guilty. You are the second person who has pointed
that out to me. What can I say? It is just one of those
totally dumb things which I do sometimes." I believe that
Salisbury was motivated by neither malice nor premedi-
tated sexism; my mother, by being a woman, just happened
to be in the wrong place at the wrong moment.

For as long as anyone can remember, my father has
called every woman who is more than ten years his junior
a girl. Since he is now ninety-one, that covers a lot of
women. He would never call a man over the age of eighteen a boy. I have tried to persuade him to mend his ways,
but the word is ingrained, and he means it gallantly. He
truly believes that inside every stout, white-haired woman
of eighty there is the glimmer of that fresh and lissome
thing, a girl.

If my father were still writing essays, every full-grown
"girl" would probably be transformed by an editor's pencil into a "woman." The same thing would happen to
E. B. White. In an essay called "The Sea and the Wind
That Blows," White described a small sailing craft as
"shaped less like a box than like a fish or a bird or a girl."

I don't think he meant a ten-year-old girl. I think he meant a girl old enough to be called a woman. But if he had compared that boat to a woman, his slim little craft, as well as his sentence, would have been forever slowed.

What I am saying here is very simple: Changing our language to make men and women equal has a cost. That doesn't mean it shouldn't be done. High prices are attached to many things that are on the whole worth doing. It does mean that the loss of our heedless grace should be mourned, and then accepted with all the civility we can muster, by every writer worth his'er salt.

During a recent visit to the Florida island where our parents live, my brother and I had dinner with them at a fancy restaurant. As we bent our heads over our menus— all of us, that is, except my father, who can't see—I realized that our identically rapt expressions had nothing to do with deciding what we wanted to eat.

"They've transposed the *e* and the *i* in Madeira sauce," commented my brother.

"They've made Bel Paese into one word," I said, "and it's lowercase."

"At least they spell better than the place where we had dinner last Tuesday," said my mother. "*They* serve P-E-A-K-I-N-G duck."

We stared at one another. You'd think that after all these decades, we Fadimans would have mapped every corner of our deviant tribal identity, but apparently there was one pan-familial gene we had never before diagnosed: we were all compulsive proofreaders.

Our confessions tumbled onto the tablecloth like so much spilled Madeira sauce. My brother revealed that in a 364-page computer-software manual he had consulted the previous month, he had found several hundred errors in spelling, grammar, and syntax. His favorite was the oft-repeated command to "insert a carrot." He had written the company, offering to trade a complete list of corrections for an upgraded version of the software, but had not received a reply. "They want to be wrong," he sighed. I knew that by "they" he meant not just the software company but everyone who was not a Fadiman.

Our mother confided that for several years she had been filling a large envelope with mistakes she had clipped from her local paper, the *Fort Myers News-Press*, with the intention of mailing them to the editor when they achieved a critical mass.

My father, who at age twenty-four had been a proof-reader—indeed, the entire proofreading department—at Simon & Schuster, admitted that in the full flush of his youthful vanity he had routinely corrected menus at posh Manhattan restaurants and handed them to the maître d's on his way out. He had even corrected *library books*, embellishing their margins with ¶s and *lc*'s and ◯s, which he viewed not as defacements but as "improvements." After he lost his sight three years ago, he had spent an insomniac night trying to figure out what kind of work he might still be capable of doing, and had hatched the following plan: He would spend twelve hours a day in front of the tele-

vision set, prooflistening for mistakes in grammar and pronunciation. He figured that if he charged five dollars a
mistake, he would become a rich man. His plan evaporated
in the harsh light of morning, however, when he decided
that, like the software company, the networks were not
Fadimans and would therefore not wish to be improved.

I myself owned up to a dark chapter from my own hu-
bristic youth. When I was twenty-three, I had discovered
fifteen misprints in the Pyramid paperback edition of Nabokov's *Speak, Memory*. (Samples: page 25, paragraph 2,
line 13: "thundercould" for "thundercloud"; page 99, paragraph 1, line 28: "acytelene" for "acetylene"; page 147,
paragraph 1, line 27, "rocco" for "rococo.") Nabokov had
always struck me as a bit of a fusspot—had he not once
observed, "In reading, one should notice and fondle details"?—so I wrote him a letter listing the errors I had
noticed and fondled, on the pretext that he could incorporate the corrections in the next edition. I deserved a kick
in the pants for my meddlesomeness, but lo and behold,
three weeks later a fragile blue aerogramme with a Swiss
postmark arrived from the Montreux-Palace Hotel. In it,
Véra Evseevna Nabokov—she who had detonated, on page
219 of the book in question, Nabokov's "slow-motion, silent
explosion of love"—thanked me on her husband's behalf
for my "thoughtfulness." Her typing was faint but 100 per-
cent error-free.

I know what you may be thinking: What an obnoxious
family! What a bunch of captious, carping, pettifogging

little busybodies! It is true—and I realize this is damning evidence—that once, when I ordered a chocolate cake to commemorate the closely proximate birthdays of my three co-Fadimans, I grabbed the order form from the bakery clerk, who had noted that it was to say "HAPPY BIRTH-DAY'S," and corrected it. I knew my family would not be distracted by the silver dragées or the pink sugar rose; had I not narrowly averted the punctuational catastrophe, they would all have cried, in chorus, "There's a superfluous apostrophe!"

Of course, if you are a compulsive proofreader yourself—and if you are, you know it, since for the afflicted it is a reflex no more avoidable than a sneeze—you are thinking something quite different: What a fine, public-spirited family are the Fadimans! How generous, in these slipshod times, to share their perspicacity with the unenlightened! If you had been alive in 1631, it would have made your day to come across the seventh commandment in the edition of the Bible specially printed for King Charles I, which read, "Thou shalt commit adultery." In 1976, if you read Beverly Sills's autobiography before it was cleaned up in the second printing, its very first sentence *did* make your day: "When I was only three and still named Belle Miriam Silverman, I sang my first aria in pubic." Your favorite part of *The New Yorker* is the column fillers. No McPhee profile, no Updike story could satisfy you as completely as the extract from the *Richmond Times-Dispatch* that read:

Meanwhile, Richard Parker Bowles, brother of Camilla's ex-husband, Andrew, said that from the beginning Camilla approved of Charles' marrying Diana while she remained his power mower.

My own power mower, George, does not understand the thrill of such discoveries. He does not think me a lovable helpmeet when I wander past his computer screen and find my fingers, as if animated by an inner gremlin, inserting a second *r* in *embarass*. I am certain, however, that the gene has passed to our six-year-old daughter. She can't yet spell well enough to correct words, but she has definitely inherited the proofreading temperament. When she was two and a half, George said to her, pointing at our bird-feeder, "Look, Susannah, a rufous towhee!" Susannah said, witheringly, "No, Daddy, a rufous-*sided* towhee." It is only a matter of time before she starts adding those missing *r*'s herself.

After our family dinner, I asked my mother if I could borrow her envelope of clippings from the *Fort Myers News-Press*. I spread them out on a table at home. There were 394. (What kind of person would count them? The daughter of the kind of person who would clip them, of course.) The offenses included fifty-six disagreements between subject and verb, eight dangling participles, three improper subjunctives, three double negatives, twelve uses of "it's" for "its," three uses of "its" for "it's," three uses of "there" for "their," three uses of "they're" for "their," and one use of "their" for "they're." Hunters shot dear; lovers exchanged martial vows; mental patients escaped from straight jackets; pianos tinkered; and Charles celebrated his twenty-fifth anniversary as the Prince of Whales. "There's a huge demographic out there," commented the *News-Press* film critic, "who appreciate good film and shouldn't be taken for granite." Even before I bumped into the large boulder at the end of that sentence, I had the feeling that I was reading a language other than English. I vowed I would never again take an intact declarative sentence for granite.

Swallowing 394 errors at a sitting gave me indigestion. One is enough. One is delicious. One is *irresistible*. My former editor John Bethell, who admits to sharing my compulsion, says that when a typo swims into his field of vision, he can't *not* notice it. He remembers his first act of proofreading—at age seven, he saw a sign in a shop window that read DIABETEC FRUIT—and recently restrained himself from correcting VINAGER on a grocery-store sign only because he feared that passersby might think he was a graffiti vandal. The Bethell family, like the Fadiman family, presents irrefutable proof that the trait is genetic. John's father, an architect, was, in effect, a proofreader of visual details. If a guest moved an ashtray a quarter of an inch, he descried the repositioning and rectified it instantly. John's daughter, Sara, manifested the gene at

an early age by stopping at dammed-up streams during
family hikes and removing all the dead leaves. Sara grew
up to be a copy editor, a profession she compares to walking
behind an elephant in a parade and scooping up what
it has left on the road. Her prize find, to date, was
a sentence in a manuscript for a San Francisco publisher:
"Einstein's Theory of Relativity led to the development of
the Big Band Theory." In her mind's ear, she still occasionally hears the strains of the cosmic orchestra.

The proofreading temperament is part of a larger syn-
drome with several interrelated symptoms, one of which is
the spotting mania. When my friend Brian Miller, also a
copy editor, was a boy, he used to sit in the woods for long
stretches, watching for subtle animal movements in the
distance. The young John Bethell was a whiz at figuring
out What's Wrong with This Picture? Proofreaders tend to
be good at distinguishing the anomalous figure—the rare
butterfly, the precious seashell—from the ordinary ground,
but, unlike collectors, we wish to discard rather than hoard.
Although not all of us are tidy, we savor certain cleaning
tasks: removing the lint from the clothes dryer, skimming
the drowned bee from the pool. My father's most treasured
possession is an enormous brass wastebasket. He is happiest
when his desktop is empty and the basket is full. One
of my brother's first sentences, a psychologically brilliant
piece of advice offered from his high chair one morning
when my father came downstairs in a grouchy mood, was
"Throw everything out, Daddy!"

Alas, there is no twelve-step program for us. We must learn to live with our affliction. Perhaps we could even attempt to extract some social benefit from it by offering our faultfinding services on a pro bono basis. Had a Fadiman or a Bethell been present in 1986, when the New York law firm of Haight, Gardner, Poor & Havens misplaced a decimal point in a ship's mortgage, we could have saved its client more than $11 million. Had we been present in 1962, when a computer programmer at NASA omitted a hyphen from *Mariner 1*'s flight program, we could have prevented the space probe from having to be destroyed when it headed off course, at a cost to taxpayers of more than $7 million.

And had we been present last year at the Tattoo Shoppe in Carlstadt, New Jersey, we could have saved Dan O'Connor, a twenty-two-year-old Notre Dame fan, from having *Fighing Irish* tattooed on his right arm. He has sued the employer of the tattooist who omitted the *t* for $250,000 in damages. I hope O'Connor wins. I can imagine few worse fates than walking around for the rest of one's life wearing a typo. As the authors of my brother's software manual would agree, it would be so hard to insert a carrot.

Thirty-three years ago, when I first laid eyes on it, my pen was already old. The barrel was a blue so uningratiatingly somber that in most lights it looked black. The cap, weathered from silver to gunmetal, had almost invisibly fine longitudinal striations and an opalescent ferrule that I imagined to be a precious jewel. The clip was gold and shaped like an arrow. To fill the pen, you unscrewed the last inch of barrel, submerged the nib in ink, and depressed a translucent plastic plunger—a sensuous advance over my previous pen's flaccid ink bladder, which made rude noises when it was squeezed.

My pen was a gift from my fifth-grade boyfriend, Jeffrey Davison, a freckled redhead who excelled at spelling bees and handball: the prototype of all the smart jocks I would fall for over the years, culminating in my husband. I have the feeling Jeffrey stole it from his stepfather, but no matter. The pen was mine by virtue of Jeffrey's love and by divine right. No one could have cherished it, for both its provenance and its attributes, more than I. Until I was in college, I reserved it for poetry—prose would have profaned it—and later, during my beginning years as a writer, I used it for every first draft. Like a dog that needs to circle three times before settling down to sleep, I could not write an opening sentence until I had uncapped the bottle of India ink, inhaled the narcotic fragrance of carbon soot and resin, dipped the nib, and pumped the plunger—one, two, three, four, five.

Muses are fickle, and many a writer, peering into the void, has escaped paralysis by ascribing the creative responsibility to a talisman: a lucky charm, a brand of paper, but most often a writing instrument. Am I writing well? Thank my pen. Am I writing badly? Don't blame me, blame my pen. By such displacements does the fearful imagination defend itself. During one dry period, Virginia Woolf wrote, "I am writing with a pen which is feeble and wispy"; during another, "What am I going to say with a defective nib?" Goethe, although he had learned elegant penmanship from a *magister artis scribendi*, dictated his great works to a copyist. This scriptorial remove only intensified his need to control the rituals of composition. He insisted that the quills be cut neither too long nor too short; that the feather plumes be removed; that the freshly inked pages be dried in front of the stove and not with sand; and that all of the above be done noiselessly, lest his concentration be broken.

Kipling was incapable of writing fiction with a pencil.

Only ink would do, the blacker the better ("all 'blue-blacks' were an abomination to my Daemon"). His favorite pen, with which he wrote *Plain Tales* in Lahore, was "a slim, octagonal-sided, agate penholder with a Waverley nib." It snapped one day, and although it was followed by a succession of dip pens, fountain pens, and pump pens, Kipling regarded these as "impersonal hirelings" and spent the rest of his life mourning the deceased Waverley.

I know how Kipling felt. Pen-bereavement is a serious matter. Ten years ago, my pen disappeared into thin air. Like a jealous lover, I never took it out of the house, so I have always believed that in rebellion against its purdah it rolled into a hidden crack in my desk. A thousand times have I been tempted to tear the desk apart; a thousand times have I resisted, fearing that the pen would not be there after all and that I would be forced to admit it was gone forever. For a time I haunted shops that sold second-hand pens, pathetically clutching an old writing sample and saying, "This is the width of the line I want." I might as well have carried a photograph of a dead lover and said, "Find me another just like this." Along the way I learned that my pen had been a Parker 51, circa 1945. Eventually I found one that matched mine not only in vintage but in color. But after this parvenu came home with me, it swung wantonly from scratching to spattering, unable, despite a series of expensive repairs, to find the silken mean its predecessor had so effortlessly achieved. Alas, it was not the reincarnation of my former love; it was a contemptible doppelgänger. Of course, I continued to write, but ever after, the feat of conjuring the first word, the first sentence, the first paragraph, has seemed more like work and less like magic.

When my friend Adam was sixteen, he bought, for twenty dollars, the letter book in which an eighteenth-century Virginia merchant had copied his correspondence: reports on the price of tobacco, orders for molasses from the West Indies, letters to loyalist friends who had fled to Nova Scotia during the Revolutionary War. Stuck between the pages were hard yellowish scraps that Adam at first took to be fingernail parings. Then he noticed that one of the scraps had the barbs of a feather attached, and he realized that they were trimmings from a quill pen: fragments of a goose that had died during the reign of George III.

How inconvenient, but how glorious, it must have been to write with a feather (preferably the second or third follicle from a bird's left wing, which curved away from a right-handed writer). An eighteenth-century inkstand—complete with quill holder, penknife, inkwell, pounce box (to hold the desiccant powder), and wafer box (to hold the paste sealing wafers)—was a monument to the physical act of writing. But if no inkstand was at hand, one could make do with temporary expedients. One day, when Sir Walter Scott was out hunting, a sentence he had been trying to compose all morning suddenly leapt into his head. Before it could fade, he shot a crow, plucked a feather, sharpened the tip, dipped it in crow's blood, and captured the sentence.

For those who consider writing a form of romance, a Parker 51 can't hold a candle to a crow's feather, but it sure beats a cartridge pen, a ballpoint, a felt-tip, or a roller-ball, especially those disposable models that proclaim, "Don't get too attached, I'm only a one-night stand." Pencils are fine in their way, but I prefer the immutability of ink. I still possess not only the poems I wrote at age ten but all the cross-outs: an even more telling index to my forgotten thought patterns. Richard Selzer, the surgeon-essayist, fills his fountain pen from a lacquered Chinese inkwell with a bronze dragon on its lid. To feed the genie that he says dwells therein, he mixes, from an old recipe, his own version of Higgins Eternal Ink, the brand he used when he learned to write sixty years ago. Eternal! To what other medium could that word possibly be applied?

A typewriter ribbon—if it's not self-correcting and if you don't use Wite-Out—may be permanent, but I would hardly call it eternal. The ichor of eternity belongs to India ink and crow's blood, not to machines. I admit the possibility, however, that typewriters, especially ancient manuals, can inspire in their owners the kind of fierce monogamy my pen inspired in me. When I worked at *Life* magazine, a veteran writer named Paul O'Neil was occasionally brought in to write crime stories. Once I saw Paul

standing at the end of one of *Life*'s long corridors, rolling
something down the carpet. It turned out he was wedded
to a typewriter so old that its ribbons were no longer available, so whenever one gave out, he held one end of the
worn-out ribbon, unspooled it with a bowler's underhand
pitch, and then painstakingly rewound a fresh ribbon, can-
nibalized from another typewriter, onto the original spool.
My mother feels the same kind of devotion to her Underwood, a venerable concatenation of levers, bars, gears,
shafts, and a tiny silver bell whose ding, tolling the end of
each line of type, hovers in the background of many of my
childhood memories. My mother is eighty. Her father
owned the typewriter before she was born. It was cleaned
and repaired once, forty years ago. In 1989, when my parents moved, it languished in storage for several months
while my mother made do with a portable Hermes. I asked
her how she felt when she retrieved the Underwood. "It
was like being reunited with a long-lost love," she said, "a
love you've been married to all your life, but until you
were parted you never realized how passionate you felt
about him."

These days I use a computer. I am using it to write this
essay, even though I should really be using a hand-whittled
crow's feather. It is, as many writers have noted, unparalleled for revision. Because it makes resequencing so easy,
it enables me to recognize structural flaws that once would
have been invisible, blocked from my imagination by the
effort and violence of the old cut-and-paste method. The

Delete key is a boon to any writer who hates a cluttered page, although it makes the word processor the least eternal of all writing instruments. Cross-outs are usually consigned to oblivion. (I prefer to move the rejected phrases to the bottom of the screen, where they are continuously pushed ahead of the text-in-progress like an ever-burgeoning mound of snow before a plow.)

I am surprised by how much I like my computer, but I will never love it. I have used several; they seem indistinguishable. When you've seen one pixel you've seen them all. As a reader, I often feel I can detect the spoor of word processing in books, particularly long ones. The writers—no longer slowed by having to change their typewriter ribbons, fill their fountain pens, or sharpen their quills—tend to be prolix. I am especially suspicious of word-processed letters, which smell of boilerplate. Word-processed addresses are even worse. What a pleasure it is to open one's mailbox and find a letter from an old friend whose handwriting on the envelope is as instantly recognizable as a face!

I recently finished writing a book. I wrote its first sentence with a pen on August 7, 1991. (I remember the date because it was my birthday.) The intervening years—during which, not coincidentally, my handwriting became virtually illegible—marked my transition from pen to word processor. I had planned to write the last page of the book in longhand, partly for the sake of sentiment, partly because I thought a pen might decelerate my prose and make me especially careful where it counted most. But when the morning finally arrived after a furious all-nighter, and I realized I was only an hour from the end, I could no more halt my pell-mell rush than a marathoner could be persuaded to sniff the roses that lined the last hundred yards of the racecourse. It was too late. My old pen may be buried somewhere in my desk, but my Daemon, who surely would never take up residence in a Compaq Deskpro 4/25 Model 120, has either fled the premises or is now—I've got my fingers crossed—living inside me.

When my son was eight months old, it could truthfully be said that he devoured literature. Presented with a book, he chewed it. A bit of Henry's DNA has been permanently incorporated into the warped pages of *Goodnight Moon*, and the missing corners of pages 3 and 8 suggest that a bit of *Goodnight Moon* has been permanently incorporated into Henry. He was, of course, not the first child to indulge in bibliophagy. The great Philadelphia bookdealer A.S.W. Rosenbach deduced that one reason first editions of *Alice in Wonderland* were so scarce was that so many of them had been eaten.

Henry and his word-swallowing colleagues—they include a *Wall Street Journal* editor who absentmindedly tears off morsels from the newsroom dictionary, rolls them in little balls, and pops them in his mouth—are merely taking literally the metaphorical similarity between reading and eating, which makes us say, for instance, that we have browsed through a newspaper or had a hard time digesting an overlong biography. When we call people bookworms, we are likening them to the larvae of insects, chiefly members of the orders *Thysanura* and *Psocoptera*, whose entire diet may consist of paper and glue. "Books are food," wrote the English critic Holbrook Jackson, "libraries so many dishes of meat, served out for several palates. . . . We eat them from love or necessity, as other foods, but most from love." Charles Lamb and Leigh Hunt were described by a friend as savoring "the flavour of a rare passage of poetry with an exquisite relish, as though it were a morsel of ripe and juicy fruit." Galileo compared *Orlando Furioso* to a melon field, Coventry Patmore compared Shakespeare to roast beef, and Edward FitzGerald compared Thucydides to Parmesan cheese.

If books are food, then books *about* food are the pièce de résistance of literary taste. Henry, who is now a year and a half, has graduated from actual page ingestion to this higher, more symbolic form of gourmandise. When he sees a picture of something toothsome, he pretends to snatch it off the page and gobble it up. He usually does this with items that are at least theoretically edible—watermelons, jars of honey, large birthday cakes—although, worrisomely, he did once try to wolf down a dental drill, which was yellow and may have resembled a banana. Later on, when Henry's diet includes novels, I expect that, like his mother, he will assess the characters not by how they look, what they wear, or how they talk, but by what they eat. In *Anna Karenina*, all the essential differences between Oblonsky and Levin are laid out in the Moscow restaurant scene during which the former orders three dozen oysters, vegetable soup, turbot with thick sauce, capon with tarragon, and fruit macédoine, while the latter longs for cabbage soup and porridge.

I have always preferred Keats to Wordsworth, but I was never able to put my finger on why until I read that Wordsworth, according to a visitor, "will live for a month on cold beef, and the next on cold bacon," whereas Keats once wrote his friend Charles Wentworth Dilke:

> Talking of Pleasure, this moment I was writing with one hand, and with the other holding to my Mouth a Nectarine—good God how fine. It went down soft, pulpy, slushy, oozy—all its delicious embonpoint melted down my throat like a large Beatified strawberry.

I have never read two sexier sentences. You just know that when Keats got together with Fanny Brawne, there must have been fireworks, just as you know, in the famous eating scene in *Tom Jones*, that Tom's appetite for Mrs. Waters will equal his appetite for his dinner, during which "three pounds at least of that flesh which formerly had contributed to the composition of an ox, was now honoured with becoming part of the individual Mr. Jones."

When I read about food, sometimes a single word is enough to detonate a chain reaction of associative memories. I am like the shoe fetishist who, in order to become aroused, no longer needs to see the object of his desire;

merely glimpsing the phrase "spectator pump, size 6½" is sufficient. Whenever I encounter the French word *plein*, which means "full," I am instantly transported back to age fifteen, when, after eating a very large portion of *poulet à l'estragon*, I told my Parisian hosts that I was "*pleine*," an adjective that I later learned is reserved for pregnant women and cows in need of milking. The word *ptarmigan* catapults me back ten years to an expedition I accompanied to the Canadian Arctic, during which a polar-bear biologist, tired of canned beans, shot a half dozen ptarmigans. We plucked them, fried them, and gnawed the bones with such ravening carnivorism that I knew on the spot I could never, ever become a vegetarian. Sometimes just the contiguous letters *pt* are enough to call up in me a nostalgic rush of guilt and greed. I may thus be the only person in the world who salivates when she reads the words "ptomaine poisoning."

My most frequent response to gastronomic references in literature is an immediate urge to raid the refrigerator. When I happen to be reading in bed, the spoils are a source of marital strife. If I had married Charles Lamb, who once told Coleridge that he was especially fond of books containing traces of buttered muffins, I would have no problem, but instead I married George, to whom crumbs on the pillows—especially *after* we have brushed our teeth— are a sign of grave moral turpitude. (I am fated to fall in love with men of the Levin rather than the Oblonsky type. Once I asked my college boyfriend what his favorite food was. He thought for a long moment, while I internally debated the relative merits of crème brûlée and runny Brie. "Well," he said, "I like bread.") But after reading M.F.K. Fisher's description of scrambled eggs in *How to Cook a Wolf*, or Hemingway's ode to sausages and potato salad in *A Moveable Feast*, or Thomas Wolfe's inventory of the contents of Joel Pierce's refrigerator in *Of Time and the River*, how could anyone in her right mind *not* bring a small snack to the matrimonial bed?

My friend Susan McCarthy, the co-author of *When Elephants Weep*, recently reminded me that reading about eating can occasionally send one running *away* from the kitchen. She mentioned a passage she had read about how killer whales feed on humpback whales. "They sort of peel them with their teeth," she explained. Susan has considered posting this passage on her refrigerator as an appetite suppressant. I could do the same with the sentence in John Lanchester's *A Debt to Pleasure* that describes a first course in a boys' boarding school as "a soup in which pieces of undisguised and unabashed gristle floated in a mud-colored sauce whose texture and temperature were powerfully reminiscent of mucus."

But I'm sure Susan and I will leave those passages right where they belong: on our bookshelves, not our refrigerators. Deep down, we know better than to subvert the glorious hunger that is whetted by the printed word. The art critic Eric Gibson once told me that one of the most frustrating experiences of his life was reading the description of chicken-and-sausage stew in *A Moment of War*, Laurie Lee's memoir of the Spanish Civil War, while riding the Washington subway, at least a half hour's ride from his kitchen.

That passage is especially powerful because the soldiers who scarfed down the stew were absolutely famished. The best food writing is associated not with decadent repletion but with hunger. Hemingway was practically starving when he ate his potato salad; Tom Jones had fasted for twenty-four hours when he indulged in his three pounds of roast beef, preparatory to indulging in Mrs. Waters. When Coleridge was a student at Christ's Hospital, where the food resembled John Lanchester's mucus soup, he liked to retreat to a sunny corner and dream of plum cake. Did he bring along *Le cuisinier royal et bourgeois*? Of course not. Wisely, he chose *Robinson Crusoe*, one of the finest hungry books in history.

In fact, my very favorite food literature does not even describe real meals. It describes meals that were *imagined* —voracious reveries by people who were hundreds of miles from the nearest larder. Accounts of Arctic and Antarctic expeditions are crammed with such figmental menus. In 1883, on Adolphus Greely's ill-fated scientific expedition to Ellesmere Island, Lieutenant James B. Lockwood kept a list of the dishes he missed most: turkey stuffed with oysters, Boston pilot bread, oatmeal muffins, corn fritters. "Chewed up a foot of a fox this evening raw," he wrote in his journal. "It was altogether bone and gristle." He

followed that entry with: "Pie of orange and coconut."
On Ernest Shackleton's 1914–17 Antarctic expedition, Dr.
James McIlroy conducted a poll of the twenty-two men
who were stranded on Elephant Island, asking each what
he would choose if he were permitted a single dish. The
sweet-cravers outnumbered the savory-cravers by a large
margin. A sampling:

Clark	Devonshire dumpling with cream
James	Syrup pudding
McIlroy	Marmalade pudding with Devonshire cream
Rickenson	Blackberry and apple tart with cream
Wild	Apple pudding and cream
Hussey	Porridge, sugar, and cream
Green	Apple dumpling
Greenstreet	Christmas pudding
Kerr	Dough and syrup
Macklin	Scrambled eggs on toast
Bakewell	Baked pork and beans
Cheetham	Pork, apple sauce, potatoes, and turnips

As a member of civilized society, the closest I've come
to these cravings has been during my pregnancies, when
the siren call of gluttony has been both irresistible and
permissible. One night, when I was pregnant with Henry,
I lay in bed thinking, for some reason, about *Treasure Island*. I realized that from the entire book there was only
one sentence I remembered verbatim, something that Ben
Gunn, who has been marooned for three years, says to Jim
Hawkins: "Many's the long night I've dreamed of cheese

—toasted, mostly." I repeated the last two words over and over, like a mantra. "Toasted, mostly. Toasted, mostly. Toasted, mostly." Then I found myself drifting toward the kitchen as if in a somnambulist's trance. I opened the refrigerator. In one of the drawers there was a lump of cheddar. I dropped it in a Teflon pan, turned up the flame, and bashed the cheese with a large spoon. This wasn't cooking, unless you call what a Neanderthal did to his haunch of woolly mammoth over a bonfire cooking. When the cheese was reduced to a molten glob, I ate it from the pan. Was it good? I don't know. It went down too fast.

Since then, I have wondered whether this in utero experience, which resulted in a terrible stomachache, was responsible for two of my son's most salient characteristics. He loves books. He hates cheese.

The editor and baseball savant Dan Okrent, who is also an excellent cook,[2] once brought a ham larded with pistachios, garlic, and raisins to a potluck lunch. The cookbook editor Judith Jones, who happened to be a guest, enjoyed it so much that she asked Dan for the recipe, which he provided verbatim from a book by James Beard. ("I thought she wanted to *cook* it," he explained later. "Not *publish* it.") When *American Food*, by Judith's husband, Evan Jones, appeared a few years later, there, on page 224,

---

1. Ecclesiastes 1:9: "The thing that hath been, it is that which shall be . . . and there is no new thing under the sun." Cf. Jean de La Bruyère, *Les Caractères* (1688): "We come too late to say anything which has not been said already." La Bruyère probably stole his line from Robert Burton's *Anatomy of Melancholy* (1621): "We can say nothing but what hath been said." Burton probably stole *his* line from Terence's *Eunuchus* (161 B.C.): "Nothing is said that has not been said before." I stole the idea of comparing these four lines from a footnote in *Bartlett's Familiar Quotations*.

2. Actually, I've never eaten anything Dan Okrent has cooked, but my friend Kathy Holub went to a dinner party at his home in 1994 and gave the pork loin high marks. I later found out that it had been cooked by Dan's wife, Becky. However, several people have assured me that Dan *could* have cooked it.

was the recipe, titled "Dan Okrent's Stuffed Fresh Ham."
Dan subsequently spotted James Beard at a cocktail party,
screwed his courage to the sticking-place,[3] and apologized
profusely. "Oh, that's all right," said Beard. "I stole the
recipe from another cookbook."[4]

In the incestuous world of cookbookery, there seems to
be no such thing as plagiarism. Add a sprig of rosemary
and the recipe is yours.[5] In literature—or so goes the con-
ventional wisdom—the rules are a bit stiffer. If you harbor
a distaste for quotation marks, if you "forget" that the el-
oquent passage you copied into your journal was really
written by Flaubert, if you delude yourself into believing
that a sprig of verbal rosemary constitutes a transfer of
ownership, then you are, as Benjamin Disraeli put it in a
famously holier-than-thou[6] phrase, "a burglar of others'
intellect."[7]

---

3. *Macbeth* (1606) 1.7.59.

4. The anecdote was stolen from Dan Okrent on October 31, 1996. The idea
of using it in the first paragraph of this essay was stolen from my husband,
George, who conceived it on November 11, 1996, while he was filling a Tup-
perware bowl with leftover spaghetti. The spaghetti recipe was from Irma S.
Rombauer and Marion Rombauer Becker's *Joy of Cooking* (1972), with emen-
dations by George's mother.

5. I stole this line from Dan Okrent. However, I made it mine by changing
"teaspoon" to "sprig."

6. Isaiah 65:5: "I am holier than thou."

7. I burglarized Disraeli's quote from the intellect of Thomas Mallon (*Stolen
Words*, 1989). As both Mallon and Alexander Lindey (*Plagiarism and Originality*,
1952) note, Disraeli's highmindedness might have rung truer had he himself not
plagiarized his funeral oration for the Duke of Wellington from Louis Adolphe
Thiers's funeral oration for General Saint-Cyr.

Like most writers, I have long been fascinated by the sea-change[8] through which an aggregation of words, common property when scattered throughout a dictionary, is transformed into a stealable asset. Neal Bowers, a poet whose work has been repeatedly plagiarized by an out-of-work schoolteacher named David Jones, has written, "The intangible nature of language begins to haunt me, and I wonder how it's possible for anyone to own words. Exactly what have I been deprived of?"[9] In other words, after your words—unlike your VCR—are stolen, you still own them. Or do you?

Bowers says you don't—or at least not in the same way. As he puts it, with justifiably ruddy temper,[10] "Who steals such words steals breath and pulse and consciousness."[11] It must have been particularly galling when another poet told Bowers that by altering the line breaks, the plagiarist had actually *improved* the poems, as if plagiarism were merely a form of editing.[12] It has long been a commonplace,

---

8. *The Tempest* (1611–12), 1.2.394.

9. Neal Bowers, "A Loss for Words," *The American Scholar* (Autumn 1994). David Jones is not named in this article; he is referred to merely as "my plagiarist," which strikes me as having a peculiar ring of proprietary intimacy, on the order of "my secretary" or "my podiatrist." Jones is identified in Bowers's book, *Words for the Taking* (1997).

10. Wallace Stevens, "The Motive for Metaphor" (1947), line 17. I think, though I'm not sure, that Stevens was talking about the temper of steel rather than of human beings, but one of the convenient things about pilfering someone else's words is that you don't have to worry about their original meaning.

11. Bowers, "A Loss for Words."

12. Ibid.

iterated with special conviction by plagiarists, that if you upgrade the original, your genius exempts you from the penalties that would be exacted from the roll of common men.[13] Virgil, well known for his sticky fingers, was once observed perusing a volume of Quintus Ennius. When asked, pointedly, what he was doing, he replied, "Plucking pearls from Ennius' dunghill."[14] Posterity may have vindicated his rummagings, since two millennia later, everyone remembers Virgil, and poor Ennius has been consigned to the dunghill of oblivion.[15]

The "poet" who plagiarized Bowers was an impostor; in order to be published, his only recourse was theft. But Virgil surely didn't need to steal from Ennius—or from Pisander or Apollonius.[16] Nor did Shakespeare really need to swipe several speeches in *Antony and Cleopatra* from Plutarch, or 4,144 of the 6,033 lines in Parts I, II, and III of *Henry VI*, either verbatim or in paraphrase, from other authors.[17] Milton didn't need to crib from Masenius,[18]

---

13. *Henry IV, Part I* (1596–97), 3.1.43.

14. I plucked this pearl from Lindey, op. cit., and upgraded it by adding the phrase "sticky fingers," which I found in *Roget's Thesaurus* under the heading "Theft."

15. Lindey said something similar about Shakespeare and the poets *he* plagiarized.

16. Lindey, op. cit.

17. I swiped these examples from Lindey, op. cit., because I needed to. The arithmetic was done by the eighteenth-century British scholar Edmond Malone.

18. Lindey notes that he borrowed his evidence from Voltaire.

Sterne from Burton,[19] or Poe from Benjamin Morrell.[20] Nor did Coleridge need to stick huge gobs of Schlegel and Schelling in his *Biographia Literaria*,[21] a theft exposed after his death by Thomas De Quincey, who was himself a plagiarist—in fact, one at least twenty times as larcenous as Coleridge.[22]

Contemplating the fact that most plagiarists don't need to steal—and also that they steal over and over again, often in such obvious ways you'd swear they wanted to get caught—I observed to my husband last month[23] that of all forms of theft, kleptomania was the one plagiarism most closely resembled. Unfortunately, I later discovered that this brilliant aperçu had already been apperceived by at least four other writers.[24] When I encountered the word

---

19. Thomas Mallon, op. cit., and Lindey, op. cit. Mallon and Lindey both note that among the passages Sterne plagiarized from Burton was a vehement denunciation of plagiarism. According to Mallon, Sterne also plagiarized from himself. He thriftily recycled several love letters he had written to his wife and, years later, sent them to his mistress.

20. Peter Shaw, "Plagiary," *The American Scholar* (Summer 1992). Shaw notes that Poe damned plagiarism as "a sickening spectacle" and falsely accused other writers of committing it.

21. Mallon, op. cit., and Shaw, op. cit. Both cite Norman Fruman's 1971 study, *Coleridge: The Damaged Archangel.* (Fruman's title was taken from an 1816 letter from Charles Lamb to William Wordsworth.)

22. Walter Jackson Bate, *Coleridge* (1973), quoted in Mallon, op. cit.

23. I can't pinpoint the date, but I know it was a Thursday, because we were unloading the dishwasher just before watching *E.R.* I cite George as a witness in order to prove that although my idea turned out to be unoriginal, I truly believed I was the first to think it.

24. Alexander Lindey, Peter Shaw, K. R. St. Onge, and Thomas Mallon.

kleptomaniac in Alexander Lindey's *Plagiarism and Originality*, I had the feeling, for a split second, that Lindey
had stolen the idea from *me*, even though his book
was written the year before I was born.[25] In any case, as
Lindey notes, the kleptomaniacal plagiarist is *compelled* to
steal. It's clear, for example, that Senator Joe Biden (or his
ghostwriters), who borrowed parts of his speeches from
Neil Kinnock, Robert Kennedy, and Hubert Humphrey,
among others, couldn't *not* plagiarize. Biden even plagiarized his apology for plagiarizing from *The Grapes of
Wrath*.[26]

The more I've read about plagiarism, the more I've come
to think that literature is one big recycling bin.[27] The sixty-
four-dollar question[28] is, how terrible is that? Before the
Romantic period, in which originality became the *summum
bonum*,[29] plagiarism was rife but viewed with far greater

---

25. Cf. Robert Merton: "Anticipatory plagiarism occurs when someone steals your
original idea and publishes it a hundred years before you were born." I am unable
to provide a citation because my source is a yellow Post-it handed to me by my
brother in Captiva, Florida, in November 1996.

26. Everything I've said about Biden is from Mallon, op. cit. Among Mallon's
other examples of Chinese-box plagiarism is Jacob Epstein's plagiarism of a description of a character's balding head from a passage that Martin Amis had
previously plagiarized from Dickens. Mallon also notes that the University of
Oregon plagiarized the section on plagiarism in its student handbook from the
section on plagiarism in Stanford's teaching-assistant handbook.

27. Cf. Alexander Pope, "Couplets on Wit" (1776), v: "Now wits gain praise by
copying other wits / As one Hog lives on what another shits."

28. From a radio quiz show first aired in 1941. The reference was suggested by
George on November 14, 1996, as he was doing his back exercises on our living
room floor.

29. Cicero, *De Officiis* (44 B.C.), 1.2.

indulgence than it is now.[30] Fielding, for example, although
he believed it was immoral to steal from his peers, wrote,
"The antients may be considered a rich common, where
every person who hath the smallest tenement in Parnassus
hath a free right to fatten his muse."[31] Even today, victims
of plagiarism, including Neal Bowers,[32] are often told that
they can always write another poem, or that imitation is
the sincerest form of flattery.[33]

I take issue with these placable attitudes because I know,
from an experience within my own family, how much
plagiarism can hurt. In 1988, I happened on a *New York
Times*[34] article that charged John Hersey with incorporating entire paragraphs from Laurence Bergreen's biography
of James Agee into his own *New Yorker* essay on the same
subject. Hersey had done a little rewriting, but Bergreen
shone through in every phrase. When I read the article, I
got a funny feeling in the pit of my stomach, because Hersey had once plagiarized from my mother.

It had happened more than forty years earlier. My
mother and her first husband, Melville Jacoby, were Far

---

30. This idea comes from Shaw, op. cit., and Harold Ogden White, *Plagiarism
and Imitation During the English Renaissance* (1965).

31. Fielding, *Tom Jones* (1749), book 12, ch. 1.

32. Bowers, op. cit.

33. Charles Caleb Colton, *Lacon* (1820–22).

34. William H. Honan, "Hersey Apologizes to a Writer over an Article on Agee,"
The New York Times (July 22, 1988).

East correspondents for *Time* during World War II. After the Japanese occupation of Manila in January of 1942, they spent three months with General Douglas MacArthur's troops on Corregidor and Bataan before escaping to Australia, where Mel was killed in an accident on an American air base. During those three months, my mother and Mel filed frequent dispatches to *Time*. They planned to base a book of their own on this material, but their dispatches instead became, without their permission, the nearly verbatim basis for about half of Hersey's best-selling *Men on Bataan*. Hersey must have had a troubled conscience, because he apparently arranged for *Time* to pay my mother and Mel $450, and—this is the most bizarre twist of all, something I didn't believe until my mother read it to me over the phone[35]—he *dedicated* the book to "Melville Jacoby, his wife Annalee," and two other journalists, "partly so they won't charge me with grand larceny."[36]

As soon as I read the *Times* article, I telephoned Larry Bergreen, with whom I'd gone to college, and told him about *Men on Bataan*. He told me that several other people, including an emeritus professor at the University of Chicago, had already called to report that, over the years, Hersey had lifted their words as well.[37] Hersey, whom Larry

35. Annalee Jacoby Fadiman, conversation with author, November 4, 1996.

36. John Hersey, *Men on Bataan* (1942).

37. Laurence Bergreen, conversation with author, summer 1988. We talked again on November 5, 1996.

had always admired as a "voice of conscience," turned out to have all the marks of the compulsive plagiarist: he borrowed repeatedly, he left extravagantly obvious clues, and —what a gifted writer he was!—he didn't need to do it.

My mother told me, "I think Hersey was ruined by the Time Inc. method of writing from correspondents' files. He just got so used to running other people's work through his typewriter and calling it his own that he started to think the whole written world was raw material."

Larry Bergreen's stolen words had, at least, been published under his own name. My mother never had that satisfaction. The only time she ever saw her dispatches in print was inside a cover that said BY JOHN HERSEY. But she wrote them. And, even though Hersey is dead and this story has long been forgotten by everyone outside our family, you can't take that away from her.[38]

---

38. Ira Gershwin, "They Can't Take That Away from Me," *Shall We Dance* (1937).

On the cover of a recent Nordstrom catalogue—don't ask me why—there is a photograph of a billy goat. He is standing on a burlap bag in the back of a pickup truck, eating a red carnation that he has just plucked from a green plastic flowerpot. The goat looks pleased with his meal, but the omnivorous glint in his eye suggests that if no carnations were available, he would be willing to settle for the burlap bag, the plastic flowerpot, or even the pickup truck.

I know that glint, because that's how I feel about reading. I'd rather have a book, but in a pinch I'll settle for a set of Water Pik instructions. I have spent many a lonely night in small-town motel rooms consoled by the Yellow Pages. Once, long ago, I bested a desperate bout of insomnia by studying the only piece of written material in my apartment that I had not already read at least twice: my roommate's 1974 Toyota Corolla manual. Under the circumstances (addiction, withdrawal, craving, panic), the section on the manual gearshift was as beautiful to me as

Dante's vision of the Sempiternal Rose in canto XXXI of the *Paradiso*.

There is only one form of non-literature, however, that I would sometimes *prefer* to the *Paradiso*. It is—I realize that I am about to deal my image a blow from which it may never recover—the mail-order catalogue. In fact, I consumed the aforementioned Nordstrom catalogue from cover to cover, even though it was downhill after the goat.

I hasten to mention that I have never actually solicited a catalogue. Although it is tempting to conclude that our mailbox hatches them by spontaneous generation, I know they are really the offspring of promiscuous mailing lists, which copulate in secret and for money. One of the pleasures, or horrors, of the direct-mail business is that you never know to whom your name will be pandered. My friend Ross Baughman, a photographer who once accompanied a group of American mercenaries to Nicaragua, inquired before the trip about a mail-order night-vision scope that would allow him to take pictures during midnight commando raids without using a flash. Ever since, he has been deluged with catalogues for pamphlets on how to make rifle silencers out of old car mufflers and napalm out of laundry detergent.

At least Ross can trace his direct-mail family tree. But why do I receive catalogues devoted exclusively to salsa, equestrian gear, electric grills, extra-large clothes, extra-small clothes, tours to sites at which UFO's have landed, and resin reproductions of medieval gargoyles? Do these companies know something about me that I don't know?

I have come to believe that the explanation turns on the fact that the address label often reads ANNE SADIMAN. (Over the phone, *F* sounds like *S*. All Fadimans have therefore learned to say, whenever we order anything, "*F* as in Frank." However, at least a quarter of the time, people think we have said, "*S* as in Srank.") Anne Fadiman is a middle-aged mother of two who possesses neither a microwave nor a CD player, let alone a deck on which to place an electric grill or a house to which such a deck might be attached. But *Anne Sadiman*——ah, she's a horse of another color, and it's almost certainly celery, blush, buff, ecru, kiwi, java, thistle, grenadine, delft, pebble, cork, or cloud, to mention a few of her favorites from the J. Crew catalogue. Wearing her Ultimate Hat from TravelSmith, which has "been crushed by Land Rovers, dropped from airplanes, and lost in raging rapids," Anne S. makes frequent trips to Lake Titicaca, the location (according to her Power Places Tours catalogue) of "one of the most powerful energy vortexes in the world." She easily attracts men (since her body has been perfected by the Macarena Workout from Collage Videos) and ladybugs (since she buys three-packs of easy-to-use, disposable Ladybug Lures from Duncraft). Courtesy of her Audio-Forum language tapes, she speaks Yupik, Xhosa, and Twi "like a diplomat." (Or better. Show me an American ambassador who is fluent in Twi and I'll eat Anne Sadiman's Ultimate Hat.) She's fond of her $1-million Diamond-Studded Miracle Bra from Victoria's

Secret, but she's equally partial to her twelve-point nickel-chrome moly steel crampons from Campmor. In fact, her husband gets particularly excited when she wears both of these items simultaneously.

Anne S.'s husband was unavailable for comment—he was on the phone with The Sharper Image, ordering her an Ultrasonic Wave Cleaner whose 42,000-wave-per-second piezo transducer will automatically bubble microdirt off her diamond bra—so I interviewed Anne F.'s husband instead. The question I posed was, "Why does your wife read mail-order catalogues?"

George looked me straight in the eye and said, "Because if something is addressed to you, it doesn't occur to you that you could throw it out. You're a bizarrely obedient person." (This is true. It is hard for me to walk on a DONT WALK sign even if there are no cars for miles. However, while waiting, I get back at it by thinking, DON'T OMIT THE APOSTROPHE.) George confessed that when he knew I had a deadline, he had on occasion triaged half the mailbox—*my catalogues!*—directly into the trash can. I counter-confessed that I had decided to write this essay just so that whenever he caught me reading a catalogue, I could say I was doing research.

I think I read catalogues for the same reason George stuffs himself with hors d'oeuvres at cocktail parties: they're free. How can he justify going out for sushi when all those lukewarm pigs-in-blankets are there for the taking? Similarly, how can I justify a stroll to the newsstand to pick up

The New York Review of Books when Alsto's Handy Helpers is right there in my mailbox, offering, among other memorable lucubrations, 103 words in praise of the Ro-Si Rotating Composter? I also read catalogues in order to further my education. Had it not been for Design Toscano Historical Reproductions for Home and Garden, I might never have learned that the three parts of a sixteenth-century close helmet are the visor, the ventail, and the beaver. Finally, I value catalogues for the privileged, and sometimes aesthetically stimulating, glimpses they afford of worlds from which I would otherwise be barred. Who could read the Garrett Wade tool catalogue without thinking, "This is a poem"? Not I. In fact, here it is. The following syllabically impeccable haiku consists entirely of items you can order by calling (800) 221-2942:

> *Joiner's mash, jack plane.*
> *Splitting froe? Bastard cut rasp!*
> *Craftsman dozuki.*

I hope you noted the Japanese touch in the final line, which refers, of course, to Item No. 49117.01, a saw whose blade "has a very smooth action with a very narrow kerf." (I am currently composing a villanelle inspired by the word *kerf.*)

It would take an epic—to which I fear my abilities as a poet are unequal—to do justice to the tools purveyed by the Sempiternal Rose of mail order, the 1902 Sears, Roe-

buck catalogue. Its offerings included twenty-two different blacksmiths' hammers, twelve watchmakers' files, and
seven cattle dehorners. Six hundred thousand people paid
fifty cents apiece to read it, not a small sum if you consider
that the same amount or less could have bought them one
four-hook corset, two turkey calls, three solid-silver thim-
bles, four boxes of foot powder, or five false mustaches.
The best thing about the Sears catalogue—a feature sadly
missing from almost all its descendants—was the thirteen-
page index. Who could read

and remain unmoved? And who could resist such blandish-
ments as "LADIES, YOU CAN BE BEAUTIFUL. No matter who you are, what your disfigurements may be, you
can make yourself as handsome as any lady in the land by
the use of our FRENCH ARSENIC WAFERS"?

Note that the estimable copywriters of Sears, Roebuck &
Co. said "You can be beautiful," not "*Be* beautiful." This

is an important distinction. The tiny bit of wiggle room
they left has since been lost, buried deep beneath the Cata-
logical Imperative:

- Cut tough toenails easily.
- Stop ugly fungus.
- Stop grinding your teeth at night.
- Stop bad breath in pets.
- Turn your home into a massage parlor.
- Enjoy bagels. Without a detour to the emergency room.
- Make 12 incredible-looking styles of paper shoes and then
  go for a walk.
- Serve up a deadly charge with the Swatter Electronic Insect
  Terminator.
- Shoot yucky green goo over 35 feet.
- Fill the plastic mold with peach flavored gelatin and a few
  hours later, out pops a flesh-toned left hand.

Even the ever-obedient Anne F. rebels. I won't!

But such boorish commands (quoted verbatim from
Healthy Living, The Sharper Image, and Brainstorms)
tarnish only the low end of the catalogue-writing spectrum. At the top, although the second person prevails, the
mood—as it was in the golden age of arsenic complexion
wafers—is declarative rather than imperative. Q.v., from
the J. Peterman catalogue: "Tonight your Lucia was the
best in a generation." "Someone may notice your resem-
blance to Ava Gardner." "You still have your alto sax."
How did they know?

The day J.P. arrives in the Fadiman-Sadiman household,

the world stops. No one is permitted to interrupt. The references to Henry James, Anna Akhmatova, and the Chogyal of Sikkim lull me into thinking I'm reading something worthwhile. The instructive excursi on Sir Francis Galton's hat (it had retractable shutters so his brain would not overheat) and the kind of shirts worn by polo-playing Persian princes in 1472 (open-necked) provide excellent fodder for dinner-party conversations. And who needs an atlas when you can master the spellings of Sylt, Krk, Sukhumi, Tetuán, Muhu, Bjugn, and Husøy just by reading your mail?

My analysis of J. Peterman's appeal is that it is a Harlequin romance for the kind of people who vacation in Krk. For example (to quote from the blurb for an ankle-length crêpe-de-Chine floral dress with leg-o'-mutton sleeves):

> He spends the morning repairing the deer fence. The next job is to start a compost pile. It's getting warm. As he takes off his flannel shirt, he observes that you are no longer reclining in the bay window reading Proust.

This paragraph makes a number of assumptions, all exceedingly pleasant:

1. I own a country house.
2. I own a deer fence.
3. I own a compost pile.
4. I have enough time to read Proust.
5. While reading Proust, I wear ankle-length dresses with leg-o'-mutton sleeves.

But I didn't order the dress. My problem—and it has made Anne F., though a devoted reader of catalogues, a faithless patron—is that I never want the item, I want the associated fantasy. I don't want the leg-o'-mutton sleeves, I want the country house, the window seat, and the Proust.

In fact, I threw out the entire Nordstrom catalogue except for the cover. Forget the clothes. After I get the country house, I want the goat.

When I was four, I liked to build castles with my father's pocket-sized, twenty-two-volume set of Trollope. My brother and I had a set of wooden blocks as well, but the Trollopes were superior: midnight blue, proportioned to fit a child's hand, and, because they were so much thinner than they were tall, perfect, as cards are, for constructing gates and drawbridges. I own them now. Before I wrote these sentences, I took down three of the volumes from my shelves, and before you could say Sir Raffle Buffle, *The Last Chronicle of Barset* had become a lintel balanced precariously atop the twin posts of *Lady Anna* and *Doctor Thorne*.

I can think of few better ways to introduce a child to books than to let her stack them, upend them, rearrange them, and get her fingerprints all over them. It's a wonder to me that the young Diana Trilling, who had to wash her hands before she extracted a volume of Twain or Balzac from her parents' glass-fronted bookcase, grew up to be a booklover. Our parents' model was the playground; her parents' model was the operating room. By buying his set of leatherbound classics en bloc from a door-to-door salesman, Trilling's father committed the additional heresy, unimaginable to us, of believing that a library could be one-size-fits-all rather than bespoke. My brother and I were able to fantasize far more extravagantly about our parents' tastes and desires, their aspirations and their vices, by scanning their bookcases than by snooping in their closets. Their selves were on their shelves.

Our father's library spanned the globe and three millennia, although it was particularly strong in English poetry and fiction of the eighteenth and nineteenth centuries. The only junk, relatively speaking, was science fiction; the only wholly extraliterary works were about wine and cheese. My favorite shelf held the books he had written himself. I liked seeing my own name up there—FADIMAN FADIMAN FADIMAN—especially around the age of five, since it was one of the first words I learned to spell. When my reading skills improved, I remember imagining that Erasmus must have looked like Ed Wynn because he had written something called *In Praise of Folly*. My brother remembers thinking (more accurately) that Kierkegaard must have been a terrifying fellow because he had written *The Sickness unto Death* and *Fear and Trembling*. And we both believed that our father, because his books did, somehow managed to incorporate both folly and terror, as well as every emotion in between.

Our mother's library was narrower, focusing almost entirely on China and the Philippines. Paging through *A Primer in the Writing of Chinese Characters* (published in Shanghai!) and *I Was on Corregidor* (it mentioned *her*!) was thrilling, like discovering one was the illegitimate offspring of Mata Hari. But the excitement was not unalloyed. Our father, who often boasted that he had never actually done anything except think, was still the same person he had been when he started collecting books in the early 1920s. He and his library had never diverged. Our mother, on the other hand, had once led a life of action. And why had she stopped? *Because she had had children.* Her books, which seemed the property of a woman I had never met, defined the size of the sacrifice my brother and I had exacted.

Between them, our parents had about seven thousand books. Whenever we moved to a new house, a carpenter would build a quarter of a mile of shelves; whenever we left, the new owners would rip them out. Other people's walls looked naked to me. Ours weren't flat white backdrops for pictures. They were works of art themselves, floor-to-ceiling mosaics whose vividly pigmented tiles were all tall skinny rectangles, pleasant to the touch and even, if one liked the dusty fragrance of old paper, to the sniff. Vladimir Nabokov once recorded in his diary that at the age of eight, his son associated the letters of the alphabet with particular colors. *C* was yellow; *F* was tan; *M* was robin's-egg blue. To this day, imprinted by the cloth-covered spines of the books that surrounded me thirty years ago, I feel certain that Sophocles is terra-cotta, Proust is dove gray, Conrad is cinnamon, Wilde is acid green, Poe is Prussian blue, Auden is indigo, and Roald Dahl is mauve.

There must be writers whose parents owned no books, and who were taken under the wing of a neighbor or teacher or librarian, but I have never met one. My daughter is seven, and some of the other second-grade parents complain that their children don't read for pleasure. When I visit their homes, the children's rooms are crammed with expensive books, but the parents' rooms are empty. Those children do not see their parents reading, as I did every day of my childhood. By contrast, when I walk into an apartment with books on the shelves, books on the bedside tables, books on the floor, and books on the toilet tank, then I know what I would see if I opened the door that says PRIVATE—GROWNUPS KEEP OUT: a child sprawled on the bed, reading.

My parents were merely passing on the legacy they had received from their own parents. When my mother moved from Utah to California at age nine, her father covered a sixteen-foot-long wall with bookcases, and her mother sheathed each shelf with nubbly beige wallpaper. My mother spent that summer reading the complete works of Dickens. My father grew up in Brooklyn in an immigrant family too poor to take him to a restaurant until he reached his teens, but not too poor to fill two black-walnut bookcases with the likes of Scott, Tolstoy, and Maupassant. "I read Ibsen when I was eight," he told me. "Even before that, Ibsen was *there.* I knew he was a great Norwegian dramatist, part of a world I was somehow moving toward." Last week he startled me by reciting, in an Irish accent, several lines spoken by Private Mulvaney in Kipling's *Soldiers Three*, which he had read (in a red edition with the title stamped in gold) eighty-five years earlier.

When I was fourteen, I noticed that the Late Augustan shelves in my father's British section contained a book that was turned spine in. Naturally, I made a beeline for it. It was *Fanny Hill.* (The effort to shield my innocent eyes was so obviously destined to backfire that a couple of years later, when I borrowed Freud's *Psychopathology of Everyday Life* from the Austrian shelf, I concluded my father had unconsciously *wanted* me to find *Fanny Hill.*) It is my opinion that parental bookcases are an excellent place for teenagers and erotica to meet for the first time, especially if the works are of high literary quality (John Cleland, Frank Harris, and Anaïs Nin, let us say, rather than Xaviera Hollander). Not only are the books easy to access, but the teenagers learn that, incredible as it may seem, their parents have sexual feelings too. *Fanny Hill* looked well thumbed.

When I asked several writers I know what books they remembered from their own parents' shelves, a high proportion were lubricious. Campbell Geeslin, a novelist and editor who grew up on a West Texas ranch, spent many hours in the embrace of *A Treasury of Art Masterpieces*, particularly the color reproduction of Manet's *Olympia*, whom he describes as "wearing nothing but a black ribbon around her throat, with her legs slightly crossed to hide the part I most wanted to see." The scholar and poet Charles Bell, whose father owned the second largest library in Mississippi, pored over the more risqué passages in Richard Burton's sixteen-volume translation of *The Thousand and One Nights*. When he inherited the set half a century ago, he discovered an oh-so-faintly penciled list of numbers on the back flyleaf of volume 4: page references to his dead father's own favorite salacities.

Those sixteen volumes now grace Charles Bell's library, one of the largest in Santa Fe. Campbell Geeslin did not inherit *A Treasury of Art Masterpieces*, only the fruitwood coffee table upon which it once reposed. He did, however, inherit the family Bible. Sixty years ago, his father read a chapter from it every night, leading Campbell to believe that Saul and David spoke with West Texas accents. During the readings, his mother sat at her dressing table, applying Pond's cold cream. "Whenever I open the Bible today," says Campbell, "I hear my father's voice and I smell my mother's face."

Some of my friends do not intend to leave their books to their children, believing that they would be a burden: a never-ending homework assignment, boxed and unboxed with every move, that would reproach the legatees from on high. I do not agree. I intend to leave my library to my children. My daughter already likes to look at our books and imagine what they might be about. (*Rabbit at Rest* is "the story of a sleepy bunny"; *One Man's Meat* is "a mystery about some men at a dinner table, and one of them gets steak but the others only get broccoli.") Someday she will read them, as I read *In Praise of Folly*, whose Holbein frontispiece of Erasmus looked nothing like Ed Wynn. My disappointment was part of growing up.

Seven years ago, when my parents moved from a large house to a small one, my brother and I divided the library overflow. My brother, who helped them pack, telephoned me from California, announcing each author as he emptied the bookcases. "Chekhov?" he asked. "Sure," I replied. "Turgenev?" "Uh"—I was mentally gauging my shelf space—"I guess not." Later, of course, I kicked myself for having spurned Turgenev. The four hundred volumes that passed to me (which included the Trollopes but, unfortunately, not *Fanny Hill*) were at first segregated on their own wall, the bibliothecal equivalent of a separate in-law apartment.

"You just don't want your father's Hemingways to be sullied by my Stephen Kings," said George accusingly.

"That's not true."

He tried another tack. "Your father wouldn't want his books to be a shrine. Didn't you say he used to let you build *castles* with them?"

This hit home. I realized that by keeping his library intact, I had hoped I might be able to keep my father, who

was then eighty-six, intact as well. It was a strategy unlikely to succeed.

So his Trollopes are now ensconced in our Victorian section, cheek by jowl with our decaying college paperbacks.
But I've been thinking of moving them to a lower shelf.
Our two-year-old son is beginning to show an interest in
building.

When Charles Dickens read aloud from *Oliver Twist* to a full house at St. James's Hall, his heart rate shot up from 72 to 124, and no wonder. First he became Fagin. His friend Charles Kent, who watched from the wings, said that for several minutes Dickens resembled "the very devil incarnate: his features distorted with rage, his penthouse eyebrows . . . working like the antennae of some deadly reptile, his whole aspect, half-vulpine, half-vulture-like, in its hungry wickedness." (It might accelerate anyone's pulse to look like a reptile, a mammal, and a bird simultaneously.) Then, after glancing at the stage directions he had written in the margins ("Shudder . . . Look Round with Terror . . . Murder coming"), Dickens became Bill Sikes, wielding an invisible club. Finally, he became Nancy, gasping, "Bill, dear Bill!" as she sank to the floor, blinded by her own blood. After bludgeoning Nancy and hanging Sikes, Dickens prostrated himself on a sofa offstage, unable to speak in consecutive sentences for a full ten minutes.

When I read *The Story of a Fierce Bad Rabbit* to my son last night, there was no one around to check my pulse. However, Beatrix Potter and Charles Dickens seem to have attended the same Violent Writers School, and when I got to the part where the man with the gun blasts off the rabbit's tail and whiskers ("BANG!"), I can tell you that Henry and I were both breathing pretty heavily. Private readings have certain advantages over public ones. We were both already prostrate, and had I been unable to speak in consecutive sentences, Henry never would have noticed. I was also able to insert editorial comments, such as "It wasn't a *real* gun." After describing "the pool of gore that quivered and danced in the sunlight," Dickens could not turn to his audience—even though a physician had forecast mass hysteria among the women—and say, "It wasn't *real* gore."

We do a lot of reading aloud in our household. If you're beginning to suspect that, like Dickens, we specialize in mayhem, I'm afraid you're right. One morning last week, I emerged from the bedroom to find Susannah crunching her Rice Krispies while her father read to her from *Boy*, in which the young Roald Dahl gets caned (twice), has his adenoids removed without anesthesia, and nearly loses his nose in a car accident.

"Read me again about how his nose was hanging by just a little tiny string," said Susannah.

Had I been a better mother, I would have said, "*After* breakfast." Instead, I joined the audience. George was once a singing waiter, accustomed to linking dramaturgy and digestion, and he attacked the dangling nose with verve. I could see why he had raked in such big tips. I could also see, with breakfast-table clarity, the truth of something I had long suspected: that *all* readings are performances, with Dickens merely hogging the histrionic extreme of a spectrum shared by every parent who has ever lulled a child to sleep with *Grandfather Twilight*. When you read silently, only the writer performs. When you read aloud, the performance is collaborative. One partner provides the words, the other the rhythm.

No stage is required, no rehearsal, not even an audience. When he was a boy, Heine read *Don Quixote* to the trees and flowers in the Palace Garden of Düsseldorf. Lamb believed that it was criminal to read Shakespeare and Milton silently, even if no one was there to listen. During the second week of a college course in Greek, I was so thrilled by mastering the alphabet that I paced up and down my dormitory room, regaling my furniture with hundreds of repetitions of the first two lines of the *Odyssey*:

Ἄνδρα μοι ἔννεπε, Μοῦσα, πολύτροπον, ὃς μάλα πολλὰ πλάγχθη, ἐπεὶ Τροίης ἱερὸν πτολίεθρον ἔπερσε·

I recognized only two words—*Muse* and *Troy*—but it didn't matter. Homer was meant to be spoken, and even though I had no idea what he was saying, I could hear the slosh of the wine-dark sea beneath each quavering dactyl.

Since the loss of his sight, my father has inhabited a Homerically aural realm. When I was a small child, he read to me constantly, specializing in Dr. Seuss. Many years later, while I was recovering from a tonsillectomy, he read me book 1 of *War and Peace*, with the result that I still associate all Russian names of more than three syllables with sore throats. Now I read to him. The generational table-turning was disorienting at first; I seemed the parent and he the child, but the child frequently corrected my pronunciation. The blind Milton did the same with his daughters, who read him Greek, Latin, Hebrew, Syriac, Italian, and French, none of which they understood. Eventually they grumbled so vehemently that they were sent out to learn embroidery instead. I read only in English, and I always enjoy it, except when I call my father with the obituary of one of his old friends. There's no getting around the intimacy of reading aloud. He cannot grieve in private, the way he could if I mailed him the scissored page. As I hear him cough softly on the other end of the line, I plug doggedly toward the list of survivors and the location of the memorial service, knowing my voice is coming between him and his friend instead of bringing them together.

"In reading aloud," wrote Holbrook Jackson, "you are greatly privileged, first to consort with all that is noble and beautiful in thought and imagination, and then to give it forth again. You adventure among masterpieces and spread the news of your discoveries. No news better worth the spreading; few things better worth sharing."

If the masterpiece you're sharing is your own, you'd better be one hell of a reader. Dickens was; the tragic actor William Charles Macready assessed the "Sikes and Nancy" reading as worth "two Macbeths." His listeners had to pony up several shillings, whereas we can hear celebrity authors read gratis at our local bookstore or, in the case of Jay McInerney, recently promoting a book called *Dressed to Kill: James Bond, the Suited Hero*, in the Saks Fifth Avenue men's designer-clothing department. On the whole, I find public readings far less interesting than private ones. Who would not have wished to eavesdrop on Pliny, who entertained guests with his own work, or on Tolstoy, who often read his day's output to his family? Or even on the endearingly narcissistic Tennyson, who once read *Maud* to the Brownings and a few other friends, stopping every few lines to murmur, "There's a wonderful touch! That's very tender! How beautiful that is!"

The most private of all readings, of course, are performed by lovers. I remember sharing my college boyfriend's narrow bed one afternoon, lying head-to-toe in order to postpone temptation until the end of the study session, handing a huge maroon edition of *The Romantic Poets* back and forth while we took turns reading from Blake's "Songs of Innocence and of Experience." We didn't get far. Seven hundred years earlier, Paolo and his sister-in-law Francesca had run into trouble doing something along the same lines:

Time and again our eyes were brought together
by the book we read; our faces flushed and paled.

They were reading *Lancelot du Lac* to each other, and when they reached Guinevere's forbidden kiss, their own fate was sealed. As Francesca discreetly put it in canto V of Dante's *Inferno*, "That day we read no further."

And where did Paolo and Francesca end up? In the second circle of Hell, the final resting place for carnal lovers, where they were tossed about eternally by a gale-force wind. Which just goes to show that like most things worth doing, reading aloud can be dangerous. In fact, just *hearing* Francesca's story was enough to make Dante pass out on the floor of Hell.

George and I, too, often pass out when we read to each other, but like most couples with small children, we are overtaken by sleep more frequently than by anything likely to land us in Dante's second circle. Choosing the right book for the marital bed is not a task to be taken lightly. Randolph Churchill insisted on reading *The Decline and Fall of the Roman Empire* to his wife Pamela, and look what happened to them. George and I tried *The Old Curiosity Shop*, but I called a halt after chapter 3 when I began to suspect what Dickens had in store for Little Nell. Then we tried *Middlemarch*, but we stalled on page 2 after George fell asleep three nights in a row during the prologue about Saint Theresa. Finally we hit upon Robert Fagles's translation of the *Odyssey*. So far, so good. We're in the middle of book 5, and we haven't missed a night.

It was lovely to hear George read the lines I used to read in Greek, lines that had faded from my memory along with most of my knowledge of the language:

Sing to me of the man, Muse, the man of twists and turns
driven time and again off course, once he had plundered
the hallowed heights of Troy.

But our journey is so slow! Reading aloud means no skipping, no skimming, no cutting to the chase. At the rate we're going, it will take us six months to get Odysseus home to Ithaca—which isn't so bad if you consider that it took him ten years. In fact, our leisurely pace may prove to have some advantages. The poem will unfold gradually, its velocity geared to Ionians of the eighth century B.C. rather than to harried modern New Yorkers, and as it progresses, it will slow us down, too. When we started, I felt we were too busy to read Homer. Now I feel we are too busy not to read him.

Our only problem is staying awake. When George catches me nodding off, he keeps me on my toes with a little judicious emendation. For instance, Telemachus may tell his old housekeeper Eurycleia:

Come, nurse,
draw me off some wine in smaller traveling jars,
mellow, the finest vintage you've been keeping,
Perhaps something in a Mouton Cadet.

As I descend still further into the Land of the Lotus-Eaters, my critical faculties descend with me. "Those suitors," I murmur languorously. "They remind me of the Cat in the Hat."

"They do?" says George.

"You know how he barges in, raids the refrigerator, eats a cake, leaves a big pink bathtub ring . . ."

"Yes," says George sleepily. "I know just what you mean."

As he leans over to kiss me good night, I do not regret having graduated from the amorous sprints of our youths. Marriage is a long-distance course, and reading aloud is a kind of romantic Gatorade formulated to invigorate the occasionally exhausted racers.

One of the obituaries I read my father three years ago was that of the Flaubert scholar Francis Steegmuller. Toward the end of his life, when his memory was failing, he and his wife, Shirley Hazzard, read aloud every day after breakfast. *The New York Times* reported: "The day before his death, Ms. Hazzard said, the couple had just finished reading Shakespeare's 'Antony and Cleopatra' to each other 'for the umpteenth time,' surrounded by the potted geraniums he loved to tend on their terrace over the Bay of Naples."

I hope George and I will be as lucky.

A few years ago I bought a secondhand book titled *On Books and the Housing of Them*. Actually, to call it a book is to stretch—or compress—the meaning of the word, since, although it was hardbound, it was only twenty-nine pages long. I dimly registered that it was written by someone named Gladstone, but it did not occur to me that he could be *that* Gladstone. What loosened my pursestrings (to the tune of eight dollars, an extortionate twenty-eight cents a page) was the topic. I have never been able to resist a book about books.

Then I lost the little volume. Or rather, it lost itself. Too slender to bear a title on its vermilion spine, *On Books and the Housing of Them* was invisibly squashed between two obese shelf-neighbors, much as a flimsy blouse on a wire hanger can disappear for months in an overstuffed closet. Then, last summer, when I pried out one of the adjacent books—the shelf was so crowded that a crowbar would have aided the operation—out tumbled the vanished ectomorph. This time I looked at it more carefully. It had been published in May of 1898, in a limited edition of five hundred, which made the eight dollars seem more conscionable. The frontispiece was a sepia portrait of an old man. His hair was white and his cheeks subsided comfortably into his jowls, but his gaze was as fierce as a raptor's. The caption read, "William Ewart Gladstone, 1809–98."

It *was* that Gladstone: four times British Prime Minister, grand old man of the Liberal Party, scholar, financier, theologian, orator, humanitarian, and thorn in the side of Benjamin Disraeli, who, when asked to define the difference between a misfortune and a calamity, replied, "If Mr. Gladstone were to fall into the Thames, it would be a misfortune. But if someone dragged him out again, it would be a calamity."

I later learned that *On Books and the Housing of Them* was originally published in 1890 in a British journal called *The Nineteenth Century*. M. F. Mansfield, a New York publisher, esteemed it highly enough to reprint the essay in what I now realize was a memorial edition. Gladstone died on May 19, 1898; my little volume was rushed into print before the end of the month. (Boot up your computers and match that, Random House.) And then the book quickly sank into an obscurity so profound that it was not even mentioned in *Gladstone*, Roy Jenkins's recent 698-page biography.

It should have been. If you wish to understand the character of both W. E. Gladstone and Victorian England, everything you need to know is contained within the small compass of *On Books and the Housing of Them.* In the index of the Jenkins biography, under "Gladstone, William Ewart, Characteristics," we find: Energy. Priggishness. Disciplined nature and control. Conceit. Probity. Neatness and passion for order. Authoritarianism. Singlemindedness. These quintessentially Victorian traits suffuse every page of Gladstone's book. The well-regulated efficiency that he desired so keenly, but often so vainly, for the British Empire, he desired equally—and achieved—within the miniature empire of his own library.

The theme of *On Books and the Housing of Them* was simple: too many books, too little space. The problem, said Gladstone, could be solved by a shelving system that might "prevent the population of Great Britain from being extruded some centuries hence into the surrounding waters by the exorbitant dimensions of their own libraries." This observation was simultaneously facetious and earnest. Gladstone had a Scotsman's natural parsimony. His diary, which he began at fifteen and abandoned at eighty-five after he was blinded by cataracts, often detailed his days down to fifteen-minute intervals: it was, in his words, "an account-book of the all-precious gift of Time." Just as his father, a canny businessman, never squandered a penny, so Gladstone never squandered a minute. James Graham, who served in the cabinet with Gladstone in the 1840s, marveled that he "could do in four hours what it took any other man sixteen to do and . . . he worked sixteen hours a day." If he stuffed into a day what would take another man a week, it was only reasonable that he should wish to stuff into a single room enough books to fill another man's house.

Here was the plan: "First, the shelves must, as a rule, be fixed; secondly, the cases, or a large part of them, should have their side against the wall, and thus, projecting into the room for a convenient distance, they should be of twice the depth needed for a single line of books, and should hold two lines, one facing each way." This was just a warm-up. It took several thousand more words to fill in the details. Gladstone's parsimony did not extend to his diction. As a parliamentary orator, he was, according to Disraeli, "inebriated with the exuberance of his own verbosity," and as a writer, he may be the only man in history to have written a long-winded twenty-nine-page book. The bookshelves that projected at right angles into the library, he declared, "should each have attached to them what I rudely term an endpiece (for want of a better name), that is, a shallow and extremely light adhering bookcase (light by reason of the shortness of the shelves), which both increases the accommodation, and makes one short side as well as the two long ones of the parallelopiped to present simply a face of books with the lines of shelf, like threads, running between the rows."

One can see why, during an 1884 cabinet meeting, Joseph Chamberlain, the president of the Board of Trade, composed this premature epitaph for the world's most anal-retentive statesman and handed it across the table to another cabinet member:

> Here lies Mr. G., who has left us repining,
> While he is, no doubt, still engaged in refining;
> And explaining distinctions to Peter and Paul,
> Who faintly protest that distinctions so small
> Were never submitted to saints to perplex them,
> Until the Prime Minister came up to vex them.

Mr. G. calculated that a library twenty by forty feet, with projecting bookcases three feet long, twelve inches deep, and nine feet high ("so that the upper shelf can be reached by the aid of a wooden stool of two steps not more than twenty inches high"), would accommodate between eighteen thousand and twenty thousand volumes. I trust his arithmetic. He had, after all, been Chancellor of the Exchequer. This shelving plan would suffice for the home of an ordinary gentleman, but for cases of extreme book-crowding, he proposed a more radical scheme in which "nearly two-thirds, or say three-fifths, of the whole cubic contents of a properly constructed apartment may be made a nearly solid mass of books." It was detailed in a footnote so extraordinary it bears quoting nearly in full:

Let us suppose a room 28 feet by 10, and a little over 9 feet high. Divide this longitudinally for a passage 4 feet wide. Let the passage project 12 to 18 inches at each end beyond the line of the wall. Let the passage ends be entirely given to either window or glass door. Twenty-four pairs of trams run across the room. On them are placed 56 bookcases, divided by the passage, reaching to the ceiling, each 3 feet broad, 12 inches deep, and separated from its neighbors by an interval of 2 inches, and set on small wheels, pulleys, or rollers, to work along the trams. Strong handles on the inner side of each bookcase to draw it out into the passage. Each of these bookcases would hold 500 octavos; and a room of 28 feet by 10 would receive 25,000 volumes. A room of 40 feet by 20 (no great size) would receive 60,000.

The system of rolling shelves that Gladstone invented here is used today in the Bodleian Library's Radcliffe Camera and at *The New York Times Book Review*, among many other places. Like its author's life, it contained not a wasted cubic inch.

I have seen a photograph of Gladstone in his own library at Hawarden Castle, which he called the Temple of Peace. He sits in a wooden armchair, surrounded by leatherbound volumes on shelves that are, of course, constructed according to the principles set forth in *On Books and the Housing of Them* (the right-angle-projection plan, not the rolling-shelf plan). For forty-four years, the Temple of Peace provided a haven from his political life. Gladstone wrote the little book there between his third and fourth premierships, not long before his eightieth birthday, noting its composition in his diary on December 17, 1889, the day before he "[r]eviewed & threw into form all the points of possible amendment or change in the Plan of Irish Government &c. for my meeting with Mr. Parnell."

When the leadership of Great Britain pressed too heavily on him, Gladstone did one of three things: felled large trees with an ax; walked around London talking to prostitutes; or arranged books. It was an odd trio of diversions, especially the second, which, although its ostensible purpose was to reform fallen women, sometimes stimulated so many carnal thoughts in the reformer that he whipped himself afterward with a contrition-inducing scourge. Tree-felling also had its perils (bruised fingers, splinters in the eye). Only book arranging, which Jenkins describes as occasionally reaching the level of "frenzy," was invariably safe and satisfying. Parliament might be maddeningly resistant to Gladstone's plans for reduced defense spending or Irish Home Rule, but his books were always pliant. He never entrusted the task—an unending one, since he bought books by the cartload—to a secretary. "What man who really loves his books," he asked, "delegates to any other human being, as long as there is breath in his body, the office of inducting them into their homes?" A few months before he wrote that sentence, he had endowed a library in the village of Hawarden, moved twenty thousand of his own books there by wheelbarrow, and placed every one on the shelves himself.

I believe that books—buying them, reading them, annotating them, indexing them, housing them, and writing about them—saved Gladstone from paralyzing stress.

Without them, he might not have lived to the then-astonishing age of eighty-eight in spite of erysipelas, bronchitis, tonsillitis, indigestion, lumbago, catarrh, pneumonia, and, finally, cancer of the palate. "The book must of necessity be put into a bookcase," he wrote. "And the bookcase must be housed. And the house must be kept. And the library must be dusted, must be arranged, must be catalogued. What a vista of toil, yet not unhappy toil!"

As I contemplate the vista of my own book-choked apartment, I sometimes wonder whether the only thing that could prevent my library from extruding me onto the streets of Manhattan would be a visit from Gladstone and a few rolling shelves. We could work side by side—two happy compulsives with dust on our sleeves—and when we were finished, the little book with the red spine would have room to breathe.

On the morning of my forty-second birthday, George informed me that I was about to be spirited to a mystery destination. I followed him to the subway. We got off at Grand Central Station, where he commanded me to stand at a discreet distance during his sotto voce procurement of two round-trip tickets to somewhere. After a half-hour's ride through the Bronx and Yonkers, we disembarked at a town called Hastings-on-Hudson. What could possibly await us here? A three-star restaurant? A world-class art collection? A hot-air balloon, stocked with a magnum of Veuve Clicquot and a pound of caviar, from which we would achieve a hawk's-eye view of the Hudson Valley?

I trailed George along the sleepy main street and down a steep hill.

"We're here," he said.

Then I saw it: a weather-beaten little shop, perched on such a declivitous slope that it looked in danger of sliding into the Hudson River, with a faded blue sign over the door that said BOOKSTORE. Inside were an unkempt desk, a maze of out-of-plumb shelves, a flurry of dust motes, and 300,000 used books.

Seven hours later, we emerged from the Riverrun Bookshop carrying nineteen pounds of books. (I weighed them when we got home.)

Now you know why I married my husband. In my view, nineteen pounds of old books are at least nineteen times as delicious as one pound of fresh caviar. You may prefer Veuve Clicquot for *your* birthday, but give me (actually, you can't, because George beat you to it) a nine-dollar 1929 edition of Vincent Starrett's *Penny Wise and Book Foolish*, a tender paean to book collecting that contains the following sentence: "Every new search is a voyage to the Indies, a quest for buried treasure, a journey to the end of the rainbow; and whether or not at the end there shall be turned up a pot of gold or merely a delightful volume, there are always wonders along the way."

Not everyone likes used books. The smears, smudges, underlinings, and ossified toast scintillae left by their previous owners may strike daintier readers as a little icky, like secondhand underwear. When I was young I liked my books young as well. Virginal paperbacks, their margins a tabula rasa for narcissistic scribbles, were cheap enough to inspire minimal guilt when I wrote in them and bland enough to accept my defacements without complaint. In those days, just as I believed that age would buffet other people's bodies but not my own, so I believed my paperbacks would last forever. I was wrong on both counts. My college Penguins now explode in clouds of acidic dust when they are prized from their shelves. *Penny Wise and Book Foolish*, on the other hand, remains ravishing at the age of sixty-eight, its binding still firm and its bottle-green cover only slightly faded.

After paperbacks lost their allure, I converted to second-hand books partly because I couldn't afford new hardbacks and partly because I developed a taste for bindings assembled with thread rather than glue, type set in hot metal rather than by computer, and frontispieces protected by little sheets of tissue paper. I also began to enjoy the sensation of being a small link in a long chain of book owners. The immaculate first editions cherished by rare-book collectors—no notes, no signatures, no bookplates—now leave me cold. I have come to view margins as a literary commons with grazing room for everyone—the more, the merrier. In fact, the only old book I am likely to approach with unease is one with uncut pages. On an earlier birthday, George gave me a two-volume set of *Farthest North*, Fridtjof Nansen's account of his unsuccessful attempt to reach the North Pole by ship. The edges were unopened. As I slit them with an unpracticed fingernail, I was overcome with melancholy. These beautiful volumes had been published in 1897, and *not a single person had read them.* I had the urge to lend them to as many friends as possible in order to make up for all the caresses they had missed during their first century.

"Alas," wrote Henry Ward Beecher. "Where is human nature so weak as in the bookstore!" Mine is relatively strong at Barnes & Noble, because I know that if I resist a volume on one visit, and someone else buys it, an identical volume will pop up in its place like a plastic duck in a shooting gallery. And if I resist *that* one, there will be another day, another duck. In a secondhand bookstore, each volume is one-of-a-kind, neither replaceable from a publisher's warehouse nor visually identical to its original siblings, which have accreted individuality with every change of ownership. If I don't buy the book now, I may never have another chance. And therefore, like Beecher, who believed the temptations of drink were paltry compared with the temptations of books, I am weak.

At least my frailty places me in good company. Southey, noted one observer, could not pass a bookstall without "just running his eye over for one minute, even if the coach which was to take him to see Coleridge at Hampstead was within the time of starting." Of Macaulay, it was said there was "no one so ready to mount a ladder and scour the top shelf for quarto pamphlets, or curious literary relics of a bygone age, and come down after an hour's examination covered with dust and cobwebs, sending for a bun to take the place of his usual luncheon." And when the eighteenth-century London bookseller James Lackington was a young man, his wife sent him out on Christmas Eve with half a crown—all they had—to buy Christmas dinner. He passed an old bookshop and returned with Young's *Night Thoughts* in his pocket and no turkey under his arm. "I think I have acted wisely," he told his famished wife, "for had I bought a dinner we should have eaten it tomorrow, and the pleasure would have been soon over, but should we live fifty years longer, we shall have the *Night Thoughts* to feast upon."

When I visit a new bookstore, I demand cleanliness, computer monitors, and rigorous alphabetization. When I visit a secondhand bookstore, I prefer indifferent housekeeping, sleeping cats, and sufficient organizational chaos to fuel my fantasies of stumbling on, say, a copy of Poe's *Tamerlane*, like the one a fisherman found under a stack of agricultural tracts in a New Hampshire antiques barn in 1988 and purchased for fifteen dollars. It was auctioned at Sotheby's later that year for $198,000. I might note that people too well bred to mention money in other contexts do not hesitate, if they think they have gotten a bargain, to quote the sum they have spent for a used book. Lamb wrote Coleridge, "I have lit upon Fairfax's *Godfrey of Bullen*, for half-a-crown. Rejoice with me." And he wrote Southey, "I have picked up, too, another copy of Quarles for ninepence!!! O tempora! O lectores!" (I came across Lamb's cries of jubilation in volume 1 of *The Life and Works of Charles Lamb*, an undated two-volume "Edition de Luxe," complete with illustrations, which I purchased for fifteen dollars. Rejoice with me.)

The only problem with lugging home nineteen pounds of books from Hastings-on-Hudson was that several thousand pounds of books already overcrowded our shelves. Over the years, as our loft has come to look less and less like a home and more and more like a secondhand bookstore, I have frequently fantasized about making the designation official. Wouldn't it be fun, when the children are grown, to become bookdealers ourselves—"COLT & FADIMAN, Old Books Bought and Sold, Dog-Eared Volumes Our Specialty"?

Alas, I fear the reality might be a rude awakening. In a 1936 essay titled "Bookshop Memories," George Orwell recalled his days as a clerk in a secondhand bookstore. The hours were long, the shop was freezing, the shelves were strewn with dead bluebottle flies, and a large fraction of the customers were lunatics. Worst of all, the books themselves gradually lost their luster. "There was a time when I really did love books," he wrote, "loved the sight and smell and feel of them, I mean, at least if they were fifty or more years old. Nothing pleased me quite so much as to buy a job lot of them for a shilling at a country auction. . . . But as soon as I went to work in the bookshop I stopped buying books. Seen in the mass, five or ten thousand at a time, books were boring and even slightly sickening."

Was this an inevitable response, akin to the ice-cream disenchantment that reportedly overtakes every Baskin-Robbins employee, or was it (as I hoped) just Orwellian cynicism? I consulted my friend Adam, who had spent every Saturday of his sophomore and junior years at Harvard working in the Pangloss Bookshop in Cambridge. He confessed that he had been similarly disillusioned.

"I came to feel that a book without a home is a pointless thing," he said, "and in a bookshop, that's all you have. This hit me very powerfully when I visited the apartment of John Clive, the historian, after he died in 1990, to pack up his library and move it to our store. I had taken Clive's class on the British Empire that semester, but he was an unflashy lecturer and I didn't feel I'd gotten to know him. It was only when I saw his bookshelves—James Bond paperbacks cheek by jowl with nineteenth-century parliamentary proceedings—that I got a sense of who Clive really was. His intellectual furnishings explained him in a way his lectures hadn't.

"We took the books back to the store and divided them up by topic—history on the left wall, literature on the right wall, philosophy in the back alcove—and somehow, all of a sudden, they weren't John Clive anymore. Dispersing his library was like cremating a body and scattering it to the winds. I felt very sad. And I realized that books get their value from the way they coexist with the other books a person owns, and that when they lose their context, they lose their meaning.

"When I was leaving work that day, I noticed that the proprietor had put one of Clive's books in the fifty-cent cart we kept on the sidewalk. It was an Edwardian compact Shakespeare with an ugly typeface and garishly colored plates. Inside, in a round adolescent hand that must have dated from his teens or early twenties, Clive had written his name and the lines from *The Tempest* 'We are such stuff / As dreams are made on, and our little life / Is rounded with a sleep.' "

I asked Adam what he had done with the book.

"I bought it," he said, "and took it home."

Most good secondhand bookstores have a shelf labeled "Books About Books." That no such shelves exist in new bookstores is both a dispiriting reflection of readers' changing interests and an explanation of why so many of the following titles are out of print—some, in fact, for more than a century.

My favorite book about books happens to be called *The Book About Books: The Anatomy of Bibliomania*. It is a monumental compendium by Holbrook Jackson, based in form and style on Robert Burton's *Anatomy of Melancholy*, whose chapter titles alone ("Bibliopegic Dandyism"; "Symptoms of Bibliophily"; "Bibliobibacity with a Digression of Ecstasy") are whiffs of opium beckoning the book addict into a den from which he or she is likely to emerge several weeks later, tottering with intoxication. Other useful compilations of book lore and quotations include *Bookman's Pleasure*, also edited by Holbrook Jackson; *The Book-Lover's Enchiridion*, edited by Alexander Ireland; and *Books*, edited by Gerald Donaldson.

I recommend the following anthologies of essays on books and reading: *Bookworms*, edited by Laura Furman and Elinore Standard; *Reading in Bed*, edited by Steven Gilbar; *The Romance of the Book*, edited by Marshall Brooks; *The Most Wonderful Books*, edited by Michael Dorris and Emilie Buchwald; *What Is a Book?*, edited by Dale Warren; *Bouillabaisse for Bibliophiles* and *Carrousel for Bibliophiles*, both edited by William Targ; and *Men and Books*, edited by Malcolm S. MacLean and Elisabeth K. Holmes. *The Literary Gourmet*, by Linda Wolfe, is a succulent anthology of food literature, complete with recipes for Gogol's stuffed sturgeon and Maupassant's crayfish bisque. *A History of Reading*, by Alberto Manguel; *The Evolution of the Book*, by Frederick G. Kilgour; and *The Kingdom of Books*, by William Dana Orcutt, contain valuable historical material. Among the many volumes on book collecting, I am particularly fond of *Penny Wise and Book Foolish*, by Vincent Starrett, and *A Gentle Madness*, by Nicholas A. Basbanes. *ABC for Book Collectors*, John Carter's classic dictionary of book-related terms, is indispensable for the sort of reader who has always wanted to know the difference between a free endpaper and a pastedown endpaper.

Those who seek inspiration for reading aloud will find an abundance in *Charles Dickens as a Reader*, by Charles Kent, and "The Blue Room," an autobiographical essay by Adam Gopnik published in *The New Yorker* and, for reasons I can't fathom, never anthologized; "Reading Aloud," from *The Size of Thoughts*, by Nicholson Baker, focuses on the pitfalls of the art and thus cannot be classed as inspirational, but it should be read anyway because it is so funny. On the subject of arranging one's library, readers of this book will already know that I cherish *On Books and the Housing of Them*, by W. E. Gladstone.

Anyone interested in the intersection of literature and life should read *The Common Reader* and *The Second Common Reader*, by Virginia Woolf.

Six essays on books and reading have made an indelible impression on me: "On Three Kinds of Social Intercourse," from *Essays*, by Michel de Montaigne; "1808 Lectures on the Principles of Poetry," lecture 3, from *Lectures 1808–1819 on Literature*, volume 1, by Samuel Taylor Coleridge; "Detached Thoughts on Books and Reading," from *The Last Essays of Elia*, by Charles Lamb; "On Reading Old Books," from *The Plain Speaker*, by William Hazlitt; "Bookshop Memories," from *An Age Like This*, volume 1 of *The Collected Essays, Journalism, and Letters of George Orwell*; and "Unpacking My Library," from *Illuminations*, by Walter Benjamin.

❧ ACKNOWLEDGMENTS ❧

Five years ago I got a call from an editor named Stephen
G. Smith asking whether I would like to help found *Civilization*. Over the phone I could hear neither the uppercase
C nor the italics, and thus believed for a few heady moments that I was to be a latter-day Romulus, called from
my desk to get suckled by she-wolves and rout barbarians.
The truth, though it dashed my fantasies, was not altogether different. During my happy tenure there, I came to
see *Civilization*, the magazine of the Library of Congress,
as a kind of utopian city. The infinitive-splitters and the
modifier-danglers were pounding at the gate, but even
though we could hear the thump of their battering rams,
our walls were thick and our little metropolis was safe.

When I told Steve Smith I wanted to write a column
called "The Common Reader," he rashly said yes. He
informed me that I was to forget about reportage and
write about myself and my family, a fiat that was initially alarming but ultimately emancipating. The resulting

essays—some of which I've renamed or lengthened or fiddled with—became this book. Steve edited most of them, with such meticulous expertise that I was sometimes tempted to junk my own words and publish his marginalia.

I would also like to thank the members of *Civilization*'s staff—Leah Edmunds, Gretchen Ernster, Rachel Hartigan, Elizabeth Hightower, Aaron Matz, Katie O'Halleran, Diantha Parker, David Vine, and Charles Wilson—who disinterred and checked odd facts. William Mills of the Scott Polar Research Institute in Cambridge, England, provided information about Robert Falcon Scott's Antarctic base camp; Carolyn Chadwick of the Center for Book Arts, in New York City, explained how the volume I inherited from my great-grandmother was printed and bound; and P. J. Williams of St. Deiniol's Library in Hawarden, Wales, sent useful material about W. E. Gladstone's library.

At Farrar, Straus and Giroux, I was fortunate to be sheltered under the generous editorial wings of Jonathan Galassi and Natasha Wimmer. Susan Mitchell and Jonathan Lippincott made the book look beautiful, outside and in. After Karla Reganold copyedited it, I realized I wasn't nearly as good a proofreader or grammarian as I had previously thought.

Adam Goodheart deftly edited several of the essays, suggested material, and spent innumerable hours talking with me about books. Many other friends also got used to my telephone calls: "Do you dog-ear your books?" "Do you know the meaning of *opopanax*?" "What dirty books did

you steal from your parents' shelves?" Bill Abrams, Ross Baughman, Charles Bell, Laurence Bergreen, John Bethell, Sara Bethell, Lisa Colt, Sandy Colt, Byron Dobell, Lars Engle, Rob Farnsworth, Campbell Geeslin, Eric Gibson, Paula Glatzer, Peter Gradjansky, Maggie Hivnor, Kathy Holub, Rhonda Johnson, Pepe Karmel, Susan McCarthy, Charlie Monheim, Mark O'Donnell, Dan Okrent, Julie Sal-amon, Kathy Schuler, Carol Whitmore, and Sherri Yingst fielded my questions with good grace. Jon Blackman and Maud Gleason came in for more than their share of inter-rogation and were kind enough not to complain. Gary Hov-land, Robert Lescher, Brian Miller, Barbara Quarmby, Carol Sandvik, Frances Stead Sellers, and, especially, Mon-ica Gregory provided help of various kinds. My dear friends Jane Condon and Lou Ann Walker encouraged me from start to finish, as they have with all my projects for more than twenty years.

The center of this book is my family. I hope that when my children are older, Henry will forgive me for revealing that he ate part of *Goodnight Moon* and Susannah will recover from my disclosure that she thought *Rabbit at Rest* was a story about a sleepy bunny. Of the many satisfactions of parenthood, few have been keener than watching my children's faces when they open a new book for the first time.

My husband, George Howe Colt, and I courted each other with books and married each other's libraries as well as each other's selves. How lucky I was with both! George

gave every word of *Ex Libris* his close and wise editorial
attention, inspired much of it, and, most important,
whether in the Grand Canyon or in our book-filled loft in
New York City, lived it with me. What he once wrote to
me in an inscription I here write back to him, with still-
deepening love: "This is your book, too. As my life, too, is
also yours."

I began my relationship with books as a member of
Fadiman U., the insufferable foursome who never missed
a round of *College Bowl* and still proofread menus together.
If I were to rank life's pleasures, talking about books with
my brother and my parents would be close to the top. Kim
not only figures prominently in many of these essays, but
also read every word in draft and made many excellent
suggestions. My mother and father, to whom *Ex Libris* is
dedicated, read tens of thousands of pages aloud to me
when I was a child, transmitting with every syllable their
own passion for books. Because they are both writers, it
would have been easy for them to squash my literary hopes
under the weight of their unmatchable achievements, but
somehow they managed to do the opposite. Without them,
I would be neither a reader nor a writer, and I thank them
for these and many other gifts.